Dessert Boards

Dessert Boards

100+ DECADENT RECIPES
FOR ANY OCCASION

LIZ LATHAM

CIDER MILL PRESS

BOOK
PUBLISHERS

Contents

Introduction

Imagine a world where dessert reigns supreme, a place where delectable delights come together in a symphony of flavors, colors, and textures to create an unforgettable culinary experience. It is this enchanting world where dessert boards lie. And, rest assured, your journey to this realm that promises to redefine the way you enjoy and share sweet treats starts here.

Dessert boards have taken the culinary world by storm, offering a delicious twist on traditional desserts. These eye-catching and mouthwatering platters bring people together to savor, celebrate, and indulge in the sweetest of pleasures. Whether you are an experienced home baker or just looking to make a stunning impression at your next gathering, this book is your key to unlocking a world of sweetness.

In the pages that follow, you will find an endless supply of ideas and inspiration to create boards that are about more than satisfying someone's sweet tooth, supplying beautiful, decadent experiences that will leave a lasting impression on your guests and loved ones.

Best of all, creating a mouthwatering, showstopping dessert board doesn't have to be difficult. All you need is to spend a bit of time thinking about those things that will make your friends and family happy, and the approach will become clear.

Composing a dessert board is more than just collecting a bunch of confections; it is a culinary art form, a canvas for your creativity to shine. Just as a painter carefully selects colors and makes exacting strokes to bring a canvas to life, so too does the dessert board master take care while working in their medium. Should you follow that example and take similar care, every board you create will be a masterpiece in its own right, reflecting your personality and style, and appealing to your audience.

This book marks a major step on the road to such mastery, equipping you with the knowledge and skills to embark on your own journey. You will learn the secrets behind designing boards that are not only delicious but also visually stunning, all while keeping it simple.

Making an unforgettable dessert board starts with the foundation—choosing the right board or platter, whether it's made from wood to supply a rustic feel, ceramic to express elegance, or something more unique that communicates your personal style or pairs with your vision. Once you've chosen your canvas, balance becomes the next important consideration, as you want to make sure your board has a blend of flavors, textures, and colors.

From there, you move on to the star of the show, the desserts themselves. In these pages, you will find a wide range of recipes, from classic family favorites like chocolate chip cookies and mini cheesecakes to fun and delicious novelties such as a chocolate dip and strawberry fluff. Each recipe is designed to not only taste incredible but also look amazing when presented on a dessert board.

Dessert boards have an incredible versatility, making them suitable for a wide range of occasions. Whether you are hosting a casual family gathering, an elegant dinner party, or a holiday bash, you can always tailor a dessert board to fit the mood.

How to Create an Amazing Dessert Board

A successful dessert board is all about presenting an artful arrangement of delectable treats. To ensure that this happens and your guests walk away impressed, keep these helpful steps in mind.

CHOOSE YOUR BOARD: Any size or shape of board will work. Wood, ceramic, and plastic are going to be the most commonly used materials for a dessert board—keep an eye out for attractive ones at home and kitchen stores. You can also get creative and use a basket or a festive tray to hold your board.

CHOOSE YOUR THEME: Is your board intended for a holiday like Christmas or Easter? Perhaps you're celebrating a special occasion like a birthday, or the arrival of fall. Once you identify your intention, think about the flavors, colors, and shapes that you most associate with your theme—really let your imagination run.

PLAN AND GATHER YOUR DESSERTS: Now it's time to choose which types of desserts you will add. Remember that they can be homemade, store-bought, or a combination of these. You want flavors that capture your chosen theme, provide a variety of textures, colors, and sizes, and a balance of rich and light options. It's also important to take dietary restrictions, allergies, and general preferences into account when you are selecting treats, so make sure you give everyone on the guest list a bit of thought when you're putting together a board. Also, give the temperature where the board is going to be served a bit of thought—if you are putting together a board for a Fourth of July barbecue, you need to choose desserts that will keep under the hot sun.

MAKE YOUR HOMEMADE TREATS: If you choose to make some or all of the desserts that will be going on your board, make sure to schedule enough time to prepare them, and that your desserts will be at their best when you serve them. Most desserts can be stored in airtight containers for 2 to 3 days, especially if they are being refrigerated, but there are some that need to be prepared day of.

PURCHASE YOUR STORE-BOUGHT TREATS: If you are including store-bought treats to your board, plan a time to shop and identify the store(s) where you will find what you need.

DECORATIVE ELEMENTS OR PROPS: While you are shopping, keep an eye out for some decorative elements to add to your board. It can be as simple as adding a dusting of confectioners' sugar or fresh mint leaves, or a bit more thoughtful, like mini chalkboard signs that bear the names of the desserts, ornaments that match your theme, or candles.

ARRANGE YOUR DESSERTS: Once all of the treats are ready, it's time to build the board. There are no right or wrong answers in terms of arranging a spread, but there are some basics that are helpful to keep in mind.

- Start with the largest item first. This will serve as a visual anchor for the board, and from there, arranging everything else is a little easier
- Position the medium-sized treats and work your way around the board, keeping an eye on balancing colors and shapes; for example, alternating between dark chocolate truffles and colorful macarons can provide an aesthetically pleasing look
- Arrange the smallest items and then either fill in any gaps with small assorted candies, or leave a little space between the treats
- It helps to keep similar items together, like grouping all the fruit in one section and all the chocolates in another
- Also, considering using various heights to add visual appeal to your board, placing some treats in serving dishes, ramekins, or bowls

FINISHING TOUCHES: Once all of the desserts are on your board, it's time to add your finishing touches. Add garnishes and any cutlery needed for serving. Holiday-themed decorations, such as plastic spiders on a board for Halloween, also add a nice element.

STORAGE: If your board includes items that should be served cold, like ice cream or mini cheesecakes, have a plan to keep them chilled. You can also assemble the board first and leave a space open for a chilled dessert. If your spread does not have chilled items, be sure to keep every element in airtight containers until you are ready to compose your board. Covering the whole board with plastic wrap will keep it tasting fresh for a few hours before you are ready to serve.

TRANSPORTATION: When assembling a spread ahead of travelling, be sure to wrap the board with plastic wrap as tightly as possible. Placing it in a cooler or a basket can also help ensure that it arrives safely.

PRESENTATION: Let your guests know what's on the board, and consider providing them with the stories behind a few of the desserts that you made.

Spring & Summer

With all of the joy and excitement that is in the air due to the return of great weather, spring and summer are wonderful times for a dessert board. The bounty of available fresh produce makes it easy to bring balance to a board, offsetting rich items with light, vibrant fruit, and the bright sunshine means that you can let your imagination run in terms of color schemes. Just remember to take the temperature where you are going to be presenting the board into account—you'd hate to see all your hard work just melt away.

Opening Day Board

- **BABE RUTH TREATS (SEE PAGE 14)**
- **CRACKER JACKS**
- **PEANUTS**
- **SUNFLOWER SEEDS**

- **BIG LEAGUE CHEW**
- **CHOCOLATE-DIPPED PRETZELS**
- **BABY RUTH CANDY BARS**
- **ASSORTED RED AND WHITE CANDIES**

1   Choose a board, arrange all of the items on it in the desired manner, and enjoy.

Take me out to the ball game with this easy-to-put together board. Whether you want to celebrate the day that truly marks the return of spring or have a future major leaguer in your house and need to throw a baseball-themed birthday party for them, this spread is a guaranteed grand slam.

The homemade touch on this board is the Babe Ruth Treats, no-bake bars that do a great job of approximating the taste of the beloved Baby Ruth candy bars. Add in chocolate and cookie-coated pretzel rods for baseball bats and classic park treats like peanuts, Cracker Jacks, chewing gum, and sunflower seeds and you've got everything you need to celebrate America's pastime.

Babe Ruth Treats

Yield: 16 Treats / Active Time: 25 Minutes / Total Time: 1 Hour

6 cups cornflakes

1 cup chocolate chips

⅔ cup chopped unsalted roasted peanuts

1 cup creamy peanut butter

1 cup white corn syrup

½ cup packed light brown sugar

½ cup sugar

1   Line a 13 x 9–inch baking pan with parchment paper and coat it with nonstick cooking spray. In a large bowl, add the cornflakes, chocolate chips, and peanuts. Set the mixture aside.

2   In a heavy-bottomed saucepan, combine the peanut butter, corn syrup, and sugars and warm the mixture over medium heat until the sugars have dissolved and it is smooth, stirring continually.

3   Pour the peanut butter mixture over the cornflake mixture and stir until well combined.

4   Press the mixture into the prepared pan and let it cool for 10 minutes before cutting it into squares.

5   Let the treats cool completely before serving.

Easter Board

- **BUTTERCREAM FROSTING (SEE PAGE 25), FOR TOPPING**

- **BUNNY-SHAPED SUGAR COOKIES (SEE PAGE 200 FOR HOMEMADE)**

- **COCONUT FLAKES, FOR TOPPING**

- **MINIATURE MARSHMALLOWS, FOR TOPPING**

- **EDIBLE PINK GLITTER, FOR TOPPING**

- **HEART-SHAPED SPRINKLES, FOR TOPPING**

- **COLORED SPRINKLES, FOR TOPPING**

- **COCONUT COOKIES (SEE PAGE 18)**

- **FRUITY MARSHMALLOW TREATS (SEE PAGE 20)**

- **CREAM CHEESE MINTS (SEE PAGE 22)**

- **PEEPS**

- **LEMON OREO BALLS (SEE PAGE 24)**

- **ASSORTED EASTER CANDIES**

1   Spread the frosting on the sugar cookies and sprinkle coconut on top.

2   Cut the marshmallows in half diagonally and coat the cut side with the edible glitter. Use the coated marshmallows to make the bunnies' ears. Use the heart-shaped sprinkles to make the noses. Make the whiskers and eyes with colored sprinkles.

3   Choose a board, arrange the bunny cookies and remaining ingredients on it in the desired manner, and enjoy.

Here comes Peter Cottontail, hopping down the bunny trail! Perhaps he'll drop off a fun Easter basket—or, if you're truly lucky, maybe this Easter-themed board?

This board is jam-packed with the colors and tastes you associate with the arrival of spring, and you can keep the kids occupied with decorating the cookies while you work on getting the big holiday meal ready.

Coconut Cookies

Yield: 36 Cookies / Active Time: 30 Minutes / Total Time: 1 Hour and 30 Minutes

2 cups all-purpose flour

½ teaspoon kosher salt

1 teaspoon baking powder

1 tablespoon baking soda

1 cup sugar

1 cup packed brown sugar

1 cup shortening

2 large eggs, at room temperature

1 teaspoon pure vanilla extract

2 cups quick-cooking oats

2 cups cornflakes

1 cup sweetened coconut flakes

1 Preheat the oven to 350°F.

2 Line two baking sheets with parchment paper or silicone mats. In a small bowl, whisk together the flour, salt, baking powder, and baking soda. Set the mixture aside.

3 In the work bowl of a stand mixer fitted with the paddle attachment, beat the sugars and shortening until the mixture is fluffy and thoroughly combined.

4 Add the eggs and beat to incorporate them.

5 Add the vanilla and beat to incorporate.

6 With the mixer running, gradually add the dry mixture until the mixture comes together as a dough.

7 Add the oats, cornflakes, and coconut and beat to combine. The dough should be stiff.

8 Form the dough into balls and place them on the baking sheets. Place them in the oven and bake until the cookies are golden brown around the edges, 10 to 12 minutes.

9 Remove the cookies from the oven, transfer them to a wire rack, and let them cool completely before serving.

Note: To add an extra Easter touch to these cookies, place 1 cup coconut flakes in a bowl, add 2 drops of green food coloring, and toss to coat the coconut. Place some of the green coconut in the center of each cookie and top with a few chocolate eggs (if desired).

Fruity Marshmallow Treats

Yield: 9 Treats / Active Time: 15 Minutes / Total Time: 2 Hours and 15 Minutes

1¼ lbs. fruit-flavored miniature marshmallows

1½ lbs. white chocolate chips

1   Line a square 8-inch baking pan with parchment paper, making sure it overlaps the sides of the pan. Place the marshmallows in a large bowl. Set them aside.

2   Place the chocolate chips in a microwave-safe bowl and microwave for 1 minute. Remove the bowl from the microwave, stir, and then microwave in 15-second intervals until the chocolate chips are almost melted, stirring after each interval. Remove the bowl from the microwave and stir until they are smooth.

3   Pour the chocolate over the marshmallows and stir to coat.

4   Press the mixture into the baking pan, cover it with plastic wrap, and chill it in the refrigerator for 2 hours.

5   Use the parchment paper to lift the treats out of the pan. Cut them into squares and serve.

Cream Cheese Mints

Yield: 96 to 120 Mints / Active Time: 30 Minutes / Total Time: 4½ to 5½ Hours

½ lb. cream cheese, softened

5 to 6 cups confectioners' sugar

1 teaspoon peppermint extract

Various food coloring, as needed

1   Line baking sheets with parchment paper. In the work bowl of a stand mixer fitted with the paddle attachment, beat the cream cheese until it is fluffy, 2 to 3 minutes.

2   Incorporate the confectioners' sugar 1 cup at a time until the mixture has the desired consistency. You want it to be stiff and not sticky. Add the peppermint and beat to incorporate. If you are using multiple colors for the mints, divide the mixture among the necessary amount of bowls, add the food coloring, and stir to combine. Form the mixture into small balls, place them on the baking sheets, and flatten them slightly with a moistened fork.

3   Let the mints stand at room temperature and dry out for 4 to 5 hours before serving. Store any leftover mints in the refrigerator.

Lemon Oreo Balls

Yield: 28 Balls / Active Time: 40 Minutes / Total Time: 4 Hours

1 (20 oz.) package of Lemon Oreos

½ lb. cream cheese, softened

1 lb. vanilla-flavored coating chocolate

¾ lb. yellow chocolate melting wafers, for drizzling

Colored sprinkles, for topping

1   Line a baking sheet with parchment paper. Place the Oreos in a food processor and pulse until they are crushed. Add half of the cream cheese, pulse to incorporate, and then add the remaining cream cheese. Pulse to incorporate, making sure that the mixture is well combined enough to form it into balls.

2   Form the mixture into balls, place them on the baking sheet, and chill them in the refrigerator for 3 hours.

3   Line a large baking sheet with parchment paper. Break the coating chocolate into squares and place them in a microwave-safe bowl. Microwave for 1 minute. Remove the bowl from the microwave, stir, and then microwave in 15-second intervals until the chocolate is almost melted, stirring after each interval. Remove the bowl from the microwave and stir until the chocolate is smooth.

4   Remove 4 to 6 balls from the refrigerator at a time. Secure the balls with two forks and dip them into the melted chocolate until they are completely coated. Place them on the baking sheet and let the chocolate sit until it has set, about 20 minutes.

5   Place the chocolate wafers in a microwave-safe bowl and microwave for 1 minute. Remove the bowl from the microwave, stir, and then microwave in 15-second intervals until the chocolate is almost melted, stirring after each interval. Remove the bowl from the microwave and stir until the chocolate is smooth.

6   Drizzle the chocolate over the balls, decorate them with sprinkles, and let the chocolate set for 15 minutes before serving or storing in the refrigerator.

Buttercream Frosting

Yield: 4 Cups / Active Time: 10 Minutes / Total Time: 10 Minutes

1 cup unsalted butter, softened

4 cups sifted confectioners' sugar, plus more as needed

3 tablespoons whole milk, plus more as needed

1 In the work bowl of a stand mixer fitted with the paddle attachment, beat the butter until it is fluffy, 2 to 3 minutes.

2 Alternate adding 1 cup confectioners' sugar and 1 tablespoon milk, beating to incorporate between each addition. If necessary, incorporate more confectioners' sugar or milk to reach the desired consistency. Use immediately or store in the refrigerator. If storing in the refrigerator, let the frosting come to room temperature before using.

Lemon Board

- **LEMON FLUFF (SEE PAGE 28)**
- **LEMONADE COOKIES (SEE PAGE 29)**
- **LEMON OREO BALLS (SEE PAGE 24)**
- **LEMON CANDIES**
- **LEMON POCKY**

1   Choose a board, arrange all of the items on it in the desired manner, and enjoy.

Pucker up—it's time for a Lemon Board! Whether you have a lover of all things tart in your life, or you just want a fun way to celebrate the brightness and lightness that springtime has ushered back into the world. While it's definitely heavy on the lemon, there's plenty of space for you to tailor it to your own preferences by adding accompaniments, so don't hesitate to add fruit, crackers, or cookies to the spread.

Lemon Fluff

Yield: 8 Servings / Active Time: 30 Minutes / Total Time: 2 Hours

1 (3 oz.) box of Lemon Jell-O

1¾ cups boiling water

¼ cup fresh lemon juice

1 cup sugar

1 cup Cool Whip

1   Place the Jell-O and boiling water in a bowl and stir until the Jell-O has dissolved.

2   Chill the Jell-O in the refrigerator until it is starting to set, about 30 minutes.

3   In the work bowl of a stand mixer fitted with the whisk attachment, whip the Jell-O until it is fluffy. Add the lemon juice and sugar and whip until the mixture is fluffy and smooth.

4   Add the Cool Whip and fold to incorporate. Transfer the lemon fluff to a serving bowl and chill it in the refrigerator for 1 hour before serving.

Lemonade Cookies

Yield: 36 Cookies / Active Time: 30 Minutes / Total Time: 1 Hour and 30 Minutes

3 cups all-purpose flour

1 teaspoon baking soda

1 cup unsalted butter, softened

1 cup sugar, plus more for topping

2 large eggs, at room temperature

1 (6 oz.) can of frozen lemonade concentrate, thawed

1 Preheat the oven to 375°F.

2 Line two baking sheets with parchment paper or silicone mats. In a small bowl, whisk together the flour and baking soda. Set the mixture aside.

3 In the work bowl of a stand mixer fitted with the paddle attachment, cream together the butter and sugar until the mixture is light and fluffy, 4 to 5 minutes. Add the eggs and beat to incorporate.

4 Set a few tablespoons of the lemonade concentrate aside. Gradually add the dry mixture and lemonade concentrate, alternating between them, and beat until the mixture comes together as a smooth dough.

5 Form the dough into balls and place them on the baking sheets. Place the cookies in the oven and bake until they are golden brown, 8 to 10 minutes.

6 Remove the cookies from the oven, brush them with the reserved concentrate, and sprinkle sugar over the top.

7 Transfer the cookies to a wire rack and let them cool completely before serving.

Lemonade Cookies, see page 29

Beach Board

- **SAND PUDDING (SEE PAGE 34)**

- **OCEAN BARK (SEE PAGE 36)**

- **SHARK BAIT (BLUE SNACK MIX)**

- **BEACH-THEMED SUGAR COOKIES (SEE PAGE 200 FOR HOMEMADE)**

- **OCEAN-RELATED GUMMY CANDIES**

- **ASSORTED BLUE CANDIES**

1 Choose a board, arrange all of the items on it in the desired manner, and enjoy.

The perfect board to take to the shore, as kids and adults will have a blast with the buckets of Sand Pudding, and the eye-catching Ocean Bark will have everyone in awe. To make the shark bait snack mix, combine popcorn and fish gummy candies, melt some blue chocolate melting wafers, and drizzle this over the mixture. Toss to coat, and you've got an effortless snack that perfectly articulates the desired theme.

Sand Pudding

Yield: 8 to 10 Servings / Active Time: 25 Minutes / Total Time: 1 Hour and 5 Minutes

15 vanilla sandwich cookies

1 (3.4 oz.) box of instant vanilla or cheesecake pudding

2 cups whole milk

2 to 3 drops of blue food coloring

1 cup Cool Whip

Shark gummy candies, for topping

Fish gummy candies, for topping

Turtle gummy candies, for topping

Assorted candies, for topping

1   Place the sandwich cookies in a food processer and pulse until they are finely ground. Set them aside.

2   In a large bowl, whisk together the pudding and milk until the mixture is smooth. Add the food coloring and whisk to incorporate it. Chill the pudding in the refrigerator for 10 to 15 minutes.

3   Remove the pudding from the refrigerator and fold in the Cool Whip. Return the pudding to the refrigerator and chill for at least 30 minutes.

4   Place about a tablespoon of the crushed cookies in the bottom of a small, clean plastic bucket. Top it with some of the pudding, stopping at the rim of the bucket.

5   Top with more of the crushed cookies and candies. Repeat with the desired number of buckets. Store the buckets in the refrigerator until ready to serve.

Ocean Bark

Yield: 10 Servings / Active Time: 10 Minutes / Total Time: 35 Minutes

¾ lb. blue chocolate melting wafers

¾ lb. light blue chocolate melting wafers

¾ lb. white chocolate melting wafers

Colored sprinkles, for topping

Gummy sharks and fish, for topping

1 Line a large baking sheet with parchment paper. Place the blue chocolate wafers in a microwave-safe bowl and microwave for 1 minute. Remove the bowl from the microwave, stir, and then microwave in 15-second intervals until the chocolate is almost melted, stirring after each interval. Remove the bowl from the microwave and stir until the chocolate is smooth.

2 Pour the chocolate into the baking sheet and spread it with an offset spatula, making sure that it is even.

3 Place the light blue and white chocolate wafers in a microwave-safe bowl and microwave for 1 minute. Remove the bowl from the microwave, stir, and then microwave in 15-second intervals until the chocolate is almost melted, stirring after each interval. Remove the bowl from the microwave and stir until the chocolate is smooth.

4 Add spoonfuls of the light blue-and-white chocolate mixture to the melted blue chocolate and swirl with a knife.

5 Distribute the sprinkles and gummy candies over the chocolate and let the chocolate sit until it has set, about 20 minutes.

6 Break the chocolate bark into pieces and serve immediately or store in an airtight container.

Fruit Board

- **FRUIT DIP (SEE PAGE 40)**
- **CHOCOLATE DIP (SEE PAGE 42)**
- **GRAPES**
- **DRAGON FRUIT, SLICED**
- **BLACKBERRIES**
- **KIWI, PEELED AND SLICED**

- **PINEAPPLE, CHOPPED**
- **STRAWBERRIES**
- **ROSE RASPBERRIES**
- **BING AND RAINIER CHERRIES**
- **BLUEBERRIES**
- **GOOSEBERRIES**

1   Choose a board, arrange all of the items on it in the desired manner, and enjoy.

A spread consisting of various fruit is a board in itself, but when you accompany it with two luscious and easy-to-prepare dips, fruit's naturally sweet nature becomes positively transcendent. Reserve this one for those early summer days where the temperatures are getting uncomfortable and all you want to do is keep things light and fresh.

Fruit Board, *see page 37*

Fruit Dip

Yield: 3 Cups / Active Time: 10 Minutes / Total Time: 10 Minutes

½ lb. cream cheese, softened

7½ oz. marshmallow creme

2 to 3 tablespoons pineapple juice

1 In the work bowl of a stand mixer fitted with the paddle attachment, beat the cream cheese until it is fluffy, about 2 to 3 minutes.

2 Place the marshmallow creme in a microwave-safe bowl and microwave it for 10 seconds. Add the marshmallow creme to the work bowl and beat until the mixture is smooth.

3 Add the pineapple juice 1 tablespoon at a time and beat until the dip has the desired consistency. Serve immediately or store the dip in the refrigerator.

Chocolate Dip

Yield: 2 Cups / Active Time: 15 Minutes / Total Time: 15 Minutes

1 cup heavy whipping cream

1 cup semisweet or milk chocolate chips

½ lb. cream cheese, softened

1 cup sifted confectioners' sugar

1½ teaspoons pure vanilla extract

1 In the work bowl of a stand mixer fitted with the whisk attachment, beat the cream until it holds stiff peaks. Transfer the whipped cream to a clean bowl and set it aside. Wipe out the work bowl and fit the stand mixer with the paddle attachment.

2 Place the chocolate chips in a microwave-safe bowl and microwave for 1 minute. Remove the bowl from the microwave, stir, and then microwave in 15-second intervals until the chocolate chips are almost melted, stirring after each interval. Remove the chocolate from the microwave and stir until it is completely melted. Set it aside.

3 In the work bowl of the stand mixer, beat the cream cheese until it is fluffy, 2 to 3 minutes.

4 Add the confectioners' sugar and vanilla and beat until smooth.

5 Pour in the melted chocolate and beat to incorporate.

6 Add the whipping cream and fold to incorporate it. Serve immediately or store the dip in the refrigerator.

Cookies & Cream Board

- **THREE-INGREDIENT BROWNIES (SEE PAGE 48)**

- **CHOCOLATE CHIP CHEESE BALL (SEE PAGE 46)**

- **COOKIES & CREAM BARK (SEE PAGE 49)**

- **CHOCOLATE-DIPPED OREOS**

- **CHOCOLATE-DIPPED PRETZELS**

- **COOKIES & CREAM CHOCOLATE BARS**

- **OREOS**

1   Choose a board, arrange all of the items on it in the desired manner, and enjoy.

When you've got a massive cookies and cream fan in your home, as I do, it can be hard to get them excited about any other confection than that exceptional ice cream flavor. This board allows them to finally get their fill, combining a luscious chocolate-coated cheese ball, the world's easiest brownies, and a cookie-packed bark to overwhelm any cookies-and-cream craving.

Chocolate Chip Cheese Ball

Yield: 8 Servings / Active Time: 35 Minutes / Total Time: 1 Hour and 30 Minutes

½ lb. cream cheese, softened

½ cup unsalted butter, softened

½ teaspoon pure vanilla extract

¾ cup confectioners' sugar

2 tablespoons brown sugar

1 cup miniature chocolate chips, plus more for coating

Pretzels, for serving

Cookies, for serving

Graham crackers, for serving

Strawberries, for serving

1   In the work bowl of a stand mixer fitted with the paddle attachment, beat the cream cheese until fluffy, about 2 to 3 minutes.

2   Add the butter and vanilla and beat until combined.

3   Add the sugars and beat to incorporate. Add the chocolate chips and beat until they are evenly distributed.

4   Using plastic wrap, form the mixture into a ball and chill it in the refrigerator for 1 hour.

5   Place chocolate chips on a plate and roll the cheese ball in them until it is completely coated. Chill the cheese ball in the refrigerator for 30 minutes before serving with pretzels, cookies, graham crackers, and strawberries.

Three-Ingredient Brownies

Yield: 16 Brownies / Active Time: 20 Minutes / Total Time: 1 Hour and 45 Minutes

1 (15¼ oz.) box of chocolate cake mix

1 (3.4 oz.) box of cook & serve chocolate pudding

2 cups whole milk

20 chocolate sandwich cookies, broken into pieces, for topping (optional)

1 Preheat the oven to 350°F. Line a 13 x 9–inch baking pan with aluminum foil and coat it with nonstick cooking spray.

2 Place the cake mix in a large mixing bowl and set it aside.

3 In a small saucepan, combine the pudding and milk and cook over medium heat until the pudding has thickened slightly, stirring occasionally.

4 Pour the pudding into the mixing bowl and stir until well combined.

5 Spread the mixture evenly in the baking pan and top with the cookie pieces (if desired). Place the brownies in the oven and bake until a toothpick inserted into the center comes out clean, about 30 minutes.

6 Remove the brownies from the oven and let them cool completely before slicing and serving.

Cookies & Cream Bark

Yield: 10 Servings / Active Time: 10 Minutes / Total Time: 35 Minutes

1½ lbs. vanilla-flavored coating chocolate

Chocolate sandwich cookies, chopped, for topping

1 Line a large baking sheet with parchment paper. Break the coating chocolate into squares and place them in a microwave-safe bowl. Microwave for 1 minute. Remove the bowl from the microwave, stir, and then microwave in 15-second intervals until the chocolate is almost melted, stirring after each interval. Remove the bowl from the microwave and stir until the chocolate is smooth.

2 Pour the chocolate into the baking sheet and spread it with an offset spatula, making sure that it is even.

3 Distribute the cookie pieces over the chocolate and gently press down on them. Let the chocolate sit until it has set, about 20 minutes.

4 Break the chocolate bark into pieces and serve immediately or store in an airtight container.

Three-Ingredient Brownies, see page 48

Cookout Board

- **FRUIT SALSA (SEE PAGE 54)**

- **CINNAMON TORTILLA CHIPS (SEE PAGE 55)**

- **STRAWBERRY FLUFF (SEE PAGE 58)**

- **SUGAR COOKIES (SEE PAGE 200 FOR HOMEMADE), DECORATED TO RESEMBLE HAMBURGERS**

- **THREE-INGREDIENT BROWNIES (SEE PAGE 48)**

- **PUPPY CHOW (SEE PAGE 212)**

1 Choose a board, arrange all of the items on it in the desired manner, and enjoy.

Summer is the time when you gather with family and friends and spend all day laughing, soaking up the sun, and stuffing your faces. Any board of treats at a barbecue needs to focus on light and fresh flavors to counter the richness that is coming off the grill, and the Fruit Salsa, scooped up on Cinnamon Tortilla Chips, is a great way to meet that charge. With the Puppy Chow, luscious Strawberry Fluff, and cookout-themed cookies, this board will keep the cookout buzzing well into the evening.

Fruit Salsa

Yield: 5 Cups / Active Time: 35 Minutes / Total Time: 1 Hour and 45 Minutes

2 Granny Smith apples, cored and finely diced

2 tablespoons fresh lemon juice

1 cup finely diced strawberries

1 cup peeled and finely diced kiwi

1 cup finely diced pineapple

1 cup peeled and finely diced peaches

½ cup halved red raspberries

½ cup halved blackberries

¼ cup frozen limeade concentrate, thawed

2 tablespoons honey

1   Place the apples in a large mixing bowl, add the lemon juice, and toss to coat.

2   Add the remaining fruit to the bowl and gently stir to combine.

3   In a small bowl, combine the limeade and honey.

4   Pour the mixture over the fruit salsa and stir to combine.

5   Cover the bowl with plastic wrap and chill it in the refrigerator for 1 hour before serving.

Cinnamon Tortilla Chips

Yield: 4 Servings / Active Time: 15 Minutes / Total Time: 25 Minutes

¼ cup sugar

2 teaspoons cinnamon

8 flour tortillas

½ cup unsalted butter, melted

1 Preheat the oven to 400°F.

2 Line a large baking sheet with parchment paper or a silicone mat.

3 In a small bowl, combine the sugar and cinnamon. Brush both sides of the tortillas with butter and sprinkle the cinnamon sugar over them.

4 Cut the tortillas into triangles and place them on the baking sheet. Place them in the oven and bake for 3 to 4 minutes. Turn the chips over and cook until they are golden brown and crispy, 3 to 4 minutes.

5 Remove the tortilla chips from the oven and serve immediately.

Fruit Salsa, see page 54

Strawberry Fluff

Yield: 8 Servings / Active Time: 25 Minutes / Total Time: 1 Hour and 25 Minutes

1 (21 oz.) can of strawberry pie filling

1 (14 oz.) can of sweetened condensed milk

1 (20 oz.) can of crushed pineapple, drained

1 cup Cool Whip, thawed

1 cup chopped strawberries, plus more for topping

1 In a large bowl, stir the pie filling, milk, and pineapple until thoroughly combined. Add the Cool Whip and fold to combine.

2 Add the strawberries and stir until they are evenly distributed.

3 Transfer the mixture to a serving bowl and cover it with plastic wrap. Chill the strawberry fluff in the refrigerator for 1 hour.

4 Top the strawberry fluff with additional strawberries and serve.

Ice Cream Sundae Board

- **CHOCOLATE SYRUP (SEE PAGE 62)**
- **STRAWBERRY TOPPING (SEE PAGE 64)**
- **CARAMEL SAUCE (SEE PAGE 89)**
- **VARIOUS ICE CREAM FLAVORS**
- **WAFFLE CONES**
- **MARASCHINO CHERRIES**
- **COLORED SPRINKLES**
- **PEANUTS**
- **STRAWBERRIES, SLICED**
- **ASSORTED CANDIES**
- **ASSORTED COOKIES**

1   Choose a board, arrange all of the items on it in the desired manner, and enjoy.

Nothing screams summertime like ice cream! Skip the long lines, steep prices, and sticky hands that are inevitable on a trip to the local ice cream stand, and stay close to home with this decadent board that has everything you could ever want—homemade toppings, waffle cones, sprinkles, candies, and cookies so that everyone can tailor their frozen treat precisely to their taste.

Chocolate Syrup

Yield: 1 Cup / Active Time: 10 Minutes / Total Time: 25 Minutes

½ cup unsweetened cocoa powder

1 cup sugar

1 cup water

1 teaspoon pure vanilla extract

1. Combine the cocoa powder, sugar, and water in a heavy-bottomed saucepan and warm the mixture over medium heat, stirring to dissolve the sugar and cocoa powder.

2. Bring the mixture to a boil and cook for 1 minute.

3. Remove the saucepan from heat and transfer the syrup to a serving bowl. Let it cool for 15 minutes before serving.

Strawberry Topping

Yield: 2 Cups / Active Time: 10 Minutes / Total Time: 45 Minutes

2 cups hulled strawberries

1 cup sugar

3 tablespoons cornstarch

¾ cup water

1 Place the strawberries in a bowl and mash them. Set the strawberries aside.

2 In a medium saucepan, combine the sugar, cornstarch, and water and bring the mixture to a boil, stirring to dissolve the sugar and cornstarch.

3 Cook until the mixture has thickened, about 3 minutes. Stir in the strawberries, cook for 1 minute, and remove the pan from heat.

4 Let the topping cool for 15 minutes and then chill it in the refrigerator before serving.

Patriotic Board

- **CROCK-POT WHITE CHOCOLATE CANDIES (SEE PAGE 68)**

- **OREO BALLS (SEE PAGE 71)**

- **PRETZEL HUGS (SEE PAGE 70)**

- **RED LICORICE**

- **RED AND BLUE M&M'S**

- **LOLLIPOPS**

- **ROCK CANDY**

- **CHOCOLATE COINS**

- **RED MIKE & IKE CANDIES**

- **STRAWBERRIES**

- **BING CHERRIES**

1   Choose a board, arrange all of the items on it in the desired manner, and enjoy.

I had the Fourth of July in mind when I curated this board, but you should feel more than comfortable breaking it out on Memorial Day and Labor Day as well. The nice thing about this board is that it provides a nice balance between store-bought items and homemade treats, allowing you to acknowledge the sacrifices so many made before you, and actually enjoy the holiday.

Crock-Pot White Chocolate Candies

Yield: 28 to 30 Candies / Active Time: 20 Minutes / Total Time: 2 Hours and 20 Minutes

2 lbs. vanilla-flavored coating chocolate

2 cups dry-roasted peanuts

Colored sprinkles, for topping (optional)

1 Break the coating chocolate into squares and place them in a 4-quart Crock-Pot.

2 Add the peanuts, place the lid on the Crock-Pot, and cook on low for 1 hour, stirring every 15 to 20 minutes.

3 While the candy is cooking, line two large baking sheets with parchment paper.

4 Use a small scoop to scoop the candy onto the baking sheets. Top with sprinkles and let the candies set for 1 hour before serving.

Pretzel Hugs

Yield: 6 Servings / Active Time: 15 Minutes / Total Time: 1 Hour and 30 Minutes

1 (6 oz.) bag of square pretzels

1 (10.6 oz.) bag of Hershey's Hugs, unwrapped

4 pieces of vanilla-flavored coating chocolate

Colored sprinkles, for topping (optional)

1   Preheat the oven to 200°F.

2   Line a baking sheet with parchment paper.

3   Place the pretzels on the baking sheet.

4   Top the pretzels with the Hugs, place them in the oven, and bake until the Hugs are glossy and slightly melted.

5   Remove the pretzel hugs from the oven and place another pretzel on top of the melted Hugs. Let the pretzel hugs set for 30 minutes.

6   Place the coating chocolate in a microwave-safe bowl and microwave for 1 minute. Remove the bowl from the microwave, stir, and then microwave in 15-second intervals until the chocolate is almost melted, stirring after each interval. Remove the coating chocolate from the microwave and stir until the chocolate is smooth.

7   Dip one edge of each pretzel hug into the melted chocolate and top it with sprinkles (if desired). Let the white chocolate set for 20 minutes before serving.

Oreo Balls

Yield: 28 Balls / Active Time: 35 Minutes / Total Time: 4 Hours

1 (20 oz.) package of original Oreos

½ lb. cream cheese, softened

1 lb. coating chocolate (vanilla flavored or milk chocolate)

1   Line a baking sheet with parchment paper. Place the Oreos in a food processor and pulse until they are crushed. Add half of the cream cheese, pulse to incorporate, and then add the remaining cream cheese. Pulse to incorporate, making sure that the mixture is well combined enough to form it into balls.

2   Form the mixture into balls, place them on the baking sheet, and chill them in the refrigerator for 3 hours.

3   Line a large baking sheet with parchment paper. Break the coating chocolate into squares and place them in a microwave-safe bowl. Microwave for 1 minute. Remove the bowl from the microwave, stir, and then microwave in 15-second intervals until the chocolate is almost melted, stirring after each interval. Remove the bowl from the microwave and stir until the chocolate is smooth.

4   Remove 4 to 6 balls from the refrigerator at a time. Secure the balls with two forks and dip them into the melted chocolate until they are completely coated. Place them on the baking sheet and let the chocolate sit until it has set, about 20 minutes. Serve or store in the refrigerator.

Shortcake Board

- **SHORTCAKES (SEE PAGE 73)**
- **ANGEL FOOD CAKE**
- **STRAWBERRY TOPPING (SEE PAGE 64)**
- **WHIPPED CREAM**

- **STRAWBERRIES**
- **BLUEBERRIES**
- **RASPBERRIES**
- **BLACKBERRIES**

1   Choose a board, arrange all of the items on it in the desired manner, and enjoy.

Since strawberry season always feels far too brief, you need as many ways as possible to celebrate the use of their unparalleled combination of sweet and tart. This board adds yet another means, expanding one of the very best strawberry vehicles ever devised—the strawberry shortcake—to its very extreme, doubling up on the cake, including more fresh berries to add contrast and complexity, and cloaking it all in the delicious, homemade Strawberry Topping. If you've got a particularly large crew coming for the Fourth and you're worried that the Patriotic Board (see page 67) won't be enough to satisfy everyone, place this board right alongside.

Shortcakes

Yield: 8 to 10 Servings / Active Time: 30 Minutes / Total Time: 1 Hour and 15 Minutes

2 cups all-purpose flour, plus more as needed

¼ cup sugar

1 tablespoon baking powder

½ teaspoon kosher salt

½ cup unsalted butter, cubed

1 large egg

½ cup whole milk

1 Preheat the oven to 375°F.

2 Line a baking sheet with parchment paper or a silicone mat. Sift the flour, sugar, baking powder, and salt into a mixing bowl. Set the mixture aside.

3 Using a pastry blender, cut in the butter until the mixture comes together as coarse crumbs.

4 In a small bowl, beat the egg until scrambled, add the milk, and beat to incorporate.

5 Make a well in the center of the dry mixture. Add the egg mixture to the well and work the mixture until it comes together as a smooth, tacky dough.

6 Place the dough on a flour-dusted work surface and knead it until it is no longer tacky. Roll out the dough into a ½-inch-thick rectangle and cut it into rounds with a 3-inch biscuit cutter. Place the shortcakes on the baking sheet, place them in the oven, and bake until they are golden brown, 12 to 15 minutes.

7 Remove the shortcakes from the oven, transfer them to a wire rack, and let them cool completely before serving.

Shortcake Board, see page 72

Watermelon Board

- **WATERMELON PIZZA (SEE PAGE 78)**

- **FROSTED SUGAR COOKIES (SEE PAGE 200 FOR HOMEMADE), DECORATED WITH PINK FROSTING AND MINIATURE CHOCOLATE CHIPS**

- **WATERMELON RICE KRISPIES TREATS**

- **CHOCOLATE-DIPPED WATERMELON SLICES, TOPPED WITH SEA SALT**

- **ASSORTED WATERMELON-FLAVORED CANDIES**

1   Choose a board, arrange the items on it in the desired manner, and enjoy.

For many, watermelon is the ultimate sign that summertime has arrived. This board is for those folks, giving them their favorite summery flavor in all its glory, working from the Watermelon Pizza, which uses a sweet, coconut-spiked topping to highlight the fruit's fresh flavor, to the playful watermelon Rice Krispies Treats, which are easy to put together so long as you have pink and green food coloring on hand.

Watermelon Pizza

Yield: 10 Servings / Active Time: 20 Minutes / Total Time: 40 Minutes

1 seedless watermelon

½ cup cream cheese, softened

½ cup dairy-free coconut yogurt

⅓ cup confectioners' sugar

1 tablespoon orange juice

Strawberries, sliced, for topping

Peaches, sliced, for topping

Cherries, for topping

Berries, for topping

Kiwi, peeled and sliced, for topping

1 Cut the watermelon into 2-inch-thick disks. Set them aside.

2 In the work bowl of a stand mixer fitted with the paddle attachment, beat the cream cheese and yogurt until the mixture is fluffy.

3 Add the confectioners' sugar and beat to incorporate.

4 Add the orange juice and beat to incorporate. Place the mixture in the refrigerator and chill for 20 minutes.

5 Cut the watermelon into triangles and top each one with some of the cream cheese mixture. Top the slices with the fruit and serve immediately.

Fall & Winter

Energy and enthusiasm will inevitably dwindle when the days begin to grow shorter and the cold air rushes in. That is all the more reason for the dessert board master to get to work and lift their loved ones' spirits by curating comforting spreads. Luckily, these seasons are filled with plenty of momentous occasions, meaning what direction you need to head in terms of look and selection of treats is obvious. Whether you are throwing a large Christmas bash, trying to make the most of Halloween, or just snowed in, fall and winter are perfect times for a sweet spread.

Back to School Board

- **PEANUT BUTTER & JELLY CUPCAKES (SEE PAGE 84)**

- **ENERGY BALLS (SEE PAGE 86)**

- **RICE KRISPIES TREATS, DRIZZLED WITH CHOCOLATE AND DECORATED WITH ALPHABET CANDY SPRINKLES**

- **APPLE OREO POPS**

- **APPLE CHOCOLATE-DIPPED PRETZELS**

- **CHOCOLATE-DIPPED LONG SANDWICH WAFER COOKIES**

- **ANIMAL CRACKERS**

- **LETTER AND NUMBER COOKIES**

1 Choose a board, arrange all of the items on it in the desired manner, and enjoy.

If your kids are less than excited that summer is coming to an end, use this board to get them pumped about the coming school year! The Peanut Butter & Jelly Cupcakes are easily the star of the board, using a peanut butter–spiked batter and strawberry jelly to elevate the classic combo. And the apple Oreo pops are sure to get them excited about their next teacher! To make them, simply coat some Oreos in melted red chocolate wafers, insert lollipop sticks into the filling of the cookies, and use halved M&M'S for the apple's leaf and stem.

Peanut Butter & Jelly Cupcakes

Yield: 24 Cupcakes / Active Time: 35 Minutes / Total Time: 1 Hour and 30 Minutes

1   To begin preparations for the cupcakes, preheat the oven to 350°F.

2   Line a cupcake or muffin pan with cupcake liners. In a large bowl, add the cake mix, eggs, buttermilk, and canola oil and beat until the mixture comes together as a smooth batter.

3   Add the peanut butter and beat until it is thoroughly incorporated.

4   Divide the batter among the cupcake liners and place the cupcakes in the oven.

5   Bake until a toothpick inserted into their centers comes out clean, 15 to 18 minutes.

6   Remove the cupcakes from the oven and let them cool completely.

7   To begin preparations for the frosting, place the butter and peanut butter in the work bowl of a stand mixer fitted with the paddle attachment and beat until they are well combined.

8   Gradually add the confectioners' sugar and milk, alternating between them, until the desired consistency is reached. You may need to add more confectioners' sugar or more milk depending on the consistency you are looking for.

9   Transfer the frosting to a piping bag fitted with a large round tip. Pipe the frosting onto the cupcakes, top them with a small spoonful of jam, and store the cupcakes in the refrigerator until ready to serve.

For the Cupcakes

1 (15¼ oz.) box of yellow cake mix

4 large eggs, at room temperature

1 cup buttermilk, milk, or water

½ cup canola oil

¾ cup creamy peanut butter

For the Frosting

1 cup unsalted butter, softened

1 cup creamy peanut butter

2½ cups sifted confectioners' sugar, plus more as needed

3 tablespoons whole milk, plus more as needed

Strawberry jam, for topping

Note: If you would like to fill the cupcakes with jam, fill a piping bag with jam. Then, using a cupcake or apple corer, remove the center of each cupcake, being careful not to cut all the way through the bottom. Snip off the tip from the piping bag and fill the cupcakes.

Energy Balls

Yield: 50 to 60 Energy Balls / Active Time: 20 Minutes / Total Time: 50 Minutes

3 cups gluten-free oats or old-fashioned rolled oats

1½ cups almond or cashew butter, plus more as needed

1 cup honey, plus more as needed

1 tablespoon pure vanilla extract

¾ teaspoon kosher salt

3 tablespoons ground flaxseeds or hemp seeds (optional)

½ cup semisweet chocolate chips

½ cup miniature M&M'S

½ cup crushed pretzels

½ cup white chocolate chips

½ cup chopped pistachios

½ cup dried cranberries

1   In a large bowl, combine the oats, nut butter, honey, vanilla, salt, and flaxseeds (if using) and stir until the mixture is thoroughly combined.

2   Divide the mixture among 3 medium mixing bowls.

3   Mix and match the remaining ingredients, adding two of them to each portion. Stir until they are evenly distributed. If the mixtures are too dry for your liking, incorporate a little more honey or nut butter.

4   Place the mixtures in the refrigerator and chill them for 30 minutes.

5   Remove the mixtures from the refrigerator and form them into balls. Serve immediately or store in the refrigerator.

Caramel Apple Board

- **CARAMEL SAUCE (SEE PAGE 89)**

- **TAFFY APPLE COOKIE PIZZAS (SEE PAGE 92)**

- **CARAMEL APPLE CHEESECAKES (SEE PAGE 94)**

- **APPLES, SLICED, SOME DRIZZLED WITH CHOCOLATE**

- **CARAMEL CANDIES**

1 Choose a board, arrange all of the items on it in the desired manner, and enjoy.

It wouldn't be fall without a family trip to the orchard to do some apple picking. This board allows you to make the most of your haul, capitalizing on the natural affinity apples and caramel have for each other. You could, of course, just slice up a few apples, serve them alongside the Caramel Sauce, and be guaranteed a satisfying spread. But between the Caramel Apple Cheesecakes and Taffy Apple Cookie Pizzas, you're going to end up cementing those outings to the apple orchard in your children's minds forever.

Caramel Sauce

Yield: 1 Cup / Active Time: 15 Minutes / Total Time: 15 Minutes

1 cup packed light brown sugar

½ cup heavy whipping cream

¼ cup unsalted butter

Pinch of kosher salt

1 tablespoon pure vanilla extract

1 In a small saucepan, combine the brown sugar, whipping cream, butter, and salt and bring the mixture to a boil. Cook until the caramel starts to thicken, 5 to 7 minutes, swirling the pan occasionally.

2 Remove the pan from heat and stir the vanilla into the caramel.

3 Serve the caramel warm or store it in the refrigerator.

4 To reheat the caramel, place it in a microwave-safe bowl and microwave it for 20 to 30 seconds. Remove the caramel from the microwave and stir until it is smooth.

Caramel Apple Board, see page 88

Taffy Apple Cookie Pizzas

Yield: 12 to 16 Servings / Active Time: 20 Minutes / Total Time: 20 Minutes

1 to 2 Granny Smith apples, cored and sliced

1 tablespoon fresh lemon juice

½ lb. cream cheese, softened

½ cup packed light brown sugar

¼ cup creamy peanut butter

½ teaspoon pure vanilla extract

Sugar cookies (see page 200 for homemade), cooled to room temperature

Caramel Sauce (see page 89), for topping

½ cup chopped dry-roasted peanuts, for topping

1   Place the apples and lemon juice in a bowl, toss to combine, and set them aside.

2   In the work bowl of a stand mixer fitted with the paddle attachment, beat the cream cheese until it is fluffy, 2 to 3 minutes.

3   Add the brown sugar, peanut butter, and vanilla and beat until smooth.

4   Top each cookie with 1 to 2 tablespoons of the cream cheese mixture. Arrange the apple slices on top and drizzle caramel over them. Sprinkle the peanuts over the top and serve immediately.

Caramel Apple Cheesecakes

Yield: 48 Mini Cakes / Active Time: 25 Minutes / Total Time: 1 Hour and 30 Minutes

1   To begin preparations for the cheesecakes, line the wells of a miniature cupcake pan with liners.

2   Preheat the oven to 375°F.

3   Place the crushed cookies and butter in a bowl and stir until well combined. Place about ½ teaspoon of the mixture in each of the liners and use a wooden tart shaper or a spoon to press the mixture into a crust.

4   In the work bowl of a stand mixer fitted with the paddle attachment, beat the cream cheese until it is very smooth and fluffy.

5   Add the sugar, eggs, and vanilla and beat until the mixture is smooth and creamy.

6   Spoon about 1 tablespoon of the cream cheese mixture on top of each crust.

7   Place the cheesecakes in the oven and bake until they are golden brown on top, 15 to 18 minutes.

8   Keep in mind that the cheesecakes will puff up a bit in the oven, and then deflate slightly when cooled.

9   Remove the cheesecakes from the oven, transfer them to a wire rack, and let them cool completely.

10 To prepare the topping, place the butter in a small skillet and melt it over medium heat.

11 Add the apple, sugar, and cinnamon, stir to combine, and cook until the sugar starts to caramelize, 7 to 10 minutes. Transfer the mixture to a bowl and let it cool.

12 Spoon the apple mixture over the cheesecakes, drizzle caramel over them, and serve immediately.

For the Cheesecakes

40 Nilla Wafers, finely crushed

¼ cup unsalted butter, melted

1 lb. cream cheese, softened

¾ cup sugar

2 large eggs

1 teaspoon pure vanilla extract

For the Topping

3 tablespoons unsalted butter

1 large apple, peeled, cored, and finely chopped

1 tablespoon sugar

¼ teaspoon cinnamon

Caramel Sauce (see page 89)

- **CHOCOLATE CUPCAKES (SEE PAGE 98)**

- **CARAMEL SAUCE (SEE PAGE 89), FOR TOPPING**

- **BUTTERFINGERS, CHOPPED, FOR TOPPING**

- **CHOCOLATE SANDWICH COOKIES**

- **¼ CUP MELTED CHOCOLATE**

- **HOMEMADE PEANUT BUTTER CUPS (SEE PAGE 136)**

- **CANDY EYES, FOR TOPPING**

- **MINIATURE POWDERED DOUGHNUTS**

- **WHITE CHOCOLATE–DIPPED PRETZEL RODS**

- **BLACK LICORICE**

- **HALLOWEEN M&M'S**

- **CHOCOLATE EYEBALL CANDIES**

Halloween Board

1 Top the cupcakes with caramel and Butterfinger crumbles.

2 Cut the chocolate sandwich cookies in half. Spread some of the melted chocolate on the Homemade Peanut Butter Cups and affix the cookie pieces to the cups to resemble wings. Top the cookies with some melted chocolate and affix the candy eyes to them.

3 Dip some candy eyes in the melted chocolate and affix them to the powdered doughnuts.

4 Choose a board, arrange the cupcakes, cookie bats, powdered doughnuts, and remaining items on it in the desired manner, and enjoy.

All eyes are on you when Halloween rolls around. Luckily, you're more than capable of handling such scrutiny, finding the perfect balance of scrumptious and spooky with this board. While its eye-catching appearance will look like you've spent all night putting it together, the creative use of store-bought items like peanut butter cups, Oreos, and candy eyes will help ensure you keep your wits about you.

Chocolate Cupcakes

Yield: 24 Cupcakes / Active Time: 35 Minutes / Total Time: 1 Hour and 30 Minutes

2¼ cups all-purpose flour

¾ cup unsweetened cocoa powder

¾ teaspoon baking soda

½ teaspoon baking powder

½ teaspoon kosher salt

1½ cups sugar

3 large eggs, at room temperature

1¼ cups mayonnaise

1 cup hot water

⅓ cup brewed coffee

1 teaspoon pure vanilla extract

1   Preheat the oven to 350°F.

2   Line a cupcake or muffin pan with paper liners. In a small bowl, whisk together the flour, cocoa powder, baking soda, baking powder, and salt. Set the mixture aside.

3   In the work bowl of a stand mixer fitted with the paddle attachment, beat the sugar and eggs until the mixture is light and fluffy, 5 to 6 minutes.

4   Gradually add the dry mixture and the mayonnaise, alternating between them. Add the water, coffee, and vanilla and slowly stir the mixture by hand until it comes together as a smooth batter. Fill each paper liner two-thirds of the way with the batter.

5   Place the cupcakes in the oven and bake until a toothpick inserted into their centers comes out clean, 15 to 18 minutes.

6   Remove the pan from the oven and let the cupcakes cool completely before frosting them and serving.

Pie Board

- **MINIATURE PECAN PIES (SEE PAGE 102)**

- **MINIATURE PUMPKIN PIES (SEE PAGE 103)**

- **MINIATURE APPLE PIES**

- **CHOCOLATE-DIPPED PRETZELS**

- **CARAMELS**

- **MERINGUE BITES**

1 Choose a board, arrange all of the items on it in the desired manner, and enjoy.

Though any time is a good time for pie, fall is when this beloved collection of treats hits the height of its appeal. You no doubt have family and friends who are devoted to one of the classic fall pies—pecan, pumpkin, and apple—this board ensures that those folks get their fill, offering bite-size versions that will get everyone in the swing of the season. The chocolate-dipped pretzels, caramels, and meringues offer a wonderful contrast to the miniature pies, keeping everyone from being overwhelmed.

Miniature Pecan Pies

Yield: 24 Miniature Pies / Active Time: 15 Minutes / Total Time: 1 Hour and 15 Minutes

1 (14.1 oz.) box of Pillsbury Ready to Bake Pie Crusts

1 large egg

⅓ cup light corn syrup

⅓ cup sugar

1 tablespoon unsalted butter

½ teaspoon pure vanilla extract

Pinch of kosher salt

⅔ cup chopped pecans, plus whole pecans for topping

1   Preheat the oven to 350°F.

2   Cut the pie crusts into circles using a 3-inch biscuit cutter.

3   Place the crusts in the wells of a mini muffin pan. In a large bowl, whisk together the egg, corn syrup, sugar, butter, vanilla, and salt until well combined.

4   Add the chopped pecans and stir to combine.

5   Spoon the mixture into the pie crusts and place a whole pecan on top of each pie.

6   Place the pies in the oven and bake until the pie crusts are golden brown and the filling is set, 20 to 22 minutes.

7   Remove the pies from the oven, transfer them to a wire rack, and let them cool completely before serving.

Miniature Pumpkin Pies

Yield: 24 Miniature Pies / Active Time: 15 Minutes / Total Time: 1 Hour and 15 Minutes

1 (14.1 oz.) box of Pillsbury Ready to Bake Pie Crusts

1 (15 oz.) can of pumpkin puree

¾ cup sugar

1 (12 oz.) can of evaporated milk

2 large eggs

1 tablespoon pumpkin pie spice

Whipped cream, for topping

Cinnamon, for topping

1 Preheat the oven to 350°F. Cut the pie crusts into circles using a 3-inch biscuit cutter. Place the crusts in a mini muffin pan.

2 In a large bowl, whisk together the pumpkin, sugar, evaporated milk, eggs, and pumpkin pie spice until well combined.

3 Spoon the mixture into the pie crusts. Place the pies in the oven and bake until the pie crusts are golden brown and the filling is set, 20 to 22 minutes.

4 Remove the pies from the oven, transfer them to a wire rack, and let them cool completely. Top with whipped cream and a sprinkle of cinnamon before serving.

Miniature Pecan Pies, see page 102

Pink Halloween Board

- **CAKE MIX COOKIES (SEE PAGE 107)**
- **PINK GHOST CAKESICLES**
- **PINK GHOST PEEPS**
- **PINK CHOCOLATE–DIPPED PRETZELS**

- **BLACK LICORICE**
- **OREOS**
- **ASSORTED BLACK AND PINK CANDIES**

1   Choose a board, arrange all of the items on it in the desired manner, and enjoy.

While everyone loves the traditional orange and black around Halloween, that doesn't mean you shouldn't try to switch it up and extend the celebration with something new. This pink-and-black Halloween Board ensures that such an innovative attempt finds success, taking the spooky edge off the holiday and reminding everyone that the most important element of Halloween is fun.

Cake Mix Cookies

Yield: 36 to 40 Cookies / Active Time: 20 Minutes / Total Time: 1 Hour and 15 Minutes

1 (15¼ oz.) box of strawberry cake mix

2 large eggs, at room temperature

½ cup canola oil

½ cup pink sprinkles

½ cup chocolate chips

1 Preheat the oven to 350°F and line two baking sheets with parchment paper.

2 In a large bowl, beat together the cake mix, eggs, and canola oil until the mixture comes together as a smooth, thick, and sticky batter. Add the sprinkles and chocolate chips and stir until they are evenly distributed.

3 Scoop the dough onto the baking sheets and let it sit for a few minutes. Smooth the tops of the cookies with a moist finger and place them in the oven. Bake until they are just firm to the touch, 8 to 10 minutes.

4 Remove the cookies from the oven, transfer them to wire racks, and let them cool completely before serving.

Note: The strawberry cake mix is for the cookies intended for use on the Pink Halloween Board—any kind of cake mix can be used in its place, according to the situation. You should also feel free to switch up what you mix in—the chocolate chips are the best option here.

Pink Halloween Board, see page 106

Campfire Board

- **CAMPFIRE CONES (SEE PAGE 112)**
- **M&M COOKIES (SEE PAGE 256)**
- **ASSORTED CANDIES**
- **ASSORTED COOKIES**
- **GRAHAM CRACKER STICKS**

1 Choose a board, arrange all of the items on it in the desired manner, and enjoy.

Whether you are one of those who loves to head to the middle of nowhere and really rough it, or you just can't get enough of the scent of wood smoke carried on the crisp autumn air, this board will help you make the most of your time in the great outdoors. Filled with flavors that go great with the fall, easy-to-transport ingredients, and a memorable take on everyone's favorite campfire treat, the s'more, the Campfire Board will have you even more excited than normal for the arrival of every weekend.

Campfire Cones

Yield: 6 Cones / Active Time: 10 Minutes / Total Time: 20 Minutes

Miniature marshmallows

6 waffle cones

Assorted candies

Teddy Grahams

Graham crackers, broken into pieces

1   Prepare a gas or charcoal grill for medium heat (about 400°F).

2   Place a small handful of mini marshmallows in the bottom of each waffle cone. Add candies, Teddy Grahams, and graham crackers and wrap the cones in aluminum foil.

3   Place the cones on the grill and cook them for 3 to 5 minutes, turning them to ensure that they cook evenly. Remove the cones from the grill and let them cool slightly before serving.

Note: The cones can be prepared in the oven. To do this, preheat the oven to 400°F and bake them for 5 to 7 minutes.

Pumpkin Board

- **PUMPKIN & CRANBERRY COOKIES (SEE PAGE 116)**
- **PUMPKIN FLUFF (SEE PAGE 118)**
- **ASSORTED PRETZELS**
- **CHOCOLATE-COVERED PRETZELS**
- **CARAMEL CORN**
- **PUMPKIN OREOS**
- **MAPLE LEAF COOKIES**
- **NILLA WAFERS**
- **PUMPKIN-FLAVORED MERINGUES**
- **CARAMELS**
- **ASSORTED ORANGE AND BROWN CANDIES**

1   Choose a board, arrange all of the items on it in the desired manner, and enjoy.

Few flavors have exploded onto the scene quite like pumpkin over this last decade. Rich, pleasantly sweet, and able to accommodate a number of bold seasonings, pumpkin has turned out to be far more versatile than anyone could have imagined—especially when it comes to sweets. While the Pumpkin & Cranberry Cookies are the ultimate articulation of fall flavors, it is the Pumpkin Fluff that stars here, offering everything an expert dessert board curator wants: an item that is easy to prepare, full of flavor, and makes the decisions about what else to include effortless.

Pumpkin & Cranberry Cookies

Yield: 48 Cookies / Active Time: 10 Minutes / Total Time: 1 Hour and 30 Minutes

1 Preheat the oven to 350°F.

2 Line two baking sheets with parchment paper or silicone mats.

3 In a medium bowl, whisk together the flour, baking powder, cinnamon, and nutmeg. Set the mixture aside.

4 In the work bowl of a stand mixer fitted with the paddle attachment, beat the butter until it is fluffy, 4 to 5 minutes.

5 Add the brown sugar and beat until the mixture is light and fluffy.

6 Add the eggs and beat to incorporate.

7 Add the vanilla and pumpkin and beat to incorporate. Add the dry mixture and beat until the mixture comes together as a smooth dough.

8 Add the cranberries, raisins (if desired), and walnuts (if desired) and beat until they are evenly distributed. Scoop dollops of the batter onto the baking sheets, place the cookies in the oven, and bake until the cookies are golden brown around the edges, 10 to 12 minutes.

9 Remove the cookies from the oven, transfer them to a wire rack, and let them cool completely before serving.

2¼ cups all-purpose flour

4 teaspoons baking powder

½ teaspoon cinnamon

½ teaspoon freshly grated nutmeg

½ cup unsalted butter, softened

1¼ cups packed brown sugar

2 large eggs, at room temperature

1 teaspoon pure vanilla extract

1 (15 oz.) can of pure pumpkin

5 oz. dried cranberries

1 cup golden raisins (optional)

1 cup chopped walnuts (optional)

Note: Should you be looking for a bit more fall flavor, make this maple frosting: Place 3 tablespoons unsalted butter in the work bowl of a stand mixer fitted with the paddle attachment and cream until it is fluffy. Gradually add 2 cups confectioners' sugar and 1 tablespoon milk, alternating between them. Add 1 tablespoon maple syrup, beat to incorporate, and frost the cookies once they are cool.

Pumpkin Fluff

Yield: 2 Cups / Active Time: 5 Minutes / Total Time: 2 Hours and 5 Minutes

1 (15 oz.) can of pumpkin

1 cup Cool Whip, thawed

1 (3.4 oz.) box of instant vanilla pudding

2 teaspoons pumpkin pie spice

1 Place all of the ingredients in a mixing bowl and stir until well combined.

2 Transfer the mixture to a serving bowl, place it in the refrigerator, and chill for 2 hours before serving.

S'mores Board

- **S'MORE SKILLETS (SEE PAGE 121)**

- **GRAHAM CRACKERS**

- **ASSORTED COOKIES**

- **ASSORTED CHOCOLATE CANDIES**

- **ASSORTED MARSHMALLOWS**

1 Choose a board, arrange all of the items on it in the desired manner, and enjoy.

This board provides a great concept for you to employ elsewhere: the miniature cast-iron skillet. Rustic yet elegant, versatile and capable of simplifying preparations that would otherwise be a bear to prepare, these affordable and durable pieces of cookware are a must for those who love to entertain. Here, these mini skillets serve as the perfect vehicle for the gooiest elements of the s'more, cutting down on the mess considerably while still maintaining the beloved balance of flavors.

S'more Skillets

Yield: 4 Skillets / Active Time: 15 Minutes / Total Time: 15 Minutes

1 cup chocolate chips   **1 cup miniature marshmallows**

1 Preheat the oven to 375°F. Divide the chocolate chips among four small cast-iron skillets.

2 Top the chocolate chips with the marshmallows and place the pans in the oven. Bake until the marshmallows are golden brown, 5 to 10 minutes. Remove the pans from the oven, place a protective cloth or silicone sleeve on the handles of the skillets, and serve immediately.

Turkey Board

- **CHOCOLATE HUMMUS (SEE PAGE 124)**
- **2 WHITE NECCO WAFERS**
- **2 BROWN M&M'S**
- **GRANNY SMITH APPLE, DICED**
- **ORANGE AND RED STARBURSTS**
- **OATMEAL CREAM PIES**

- **LONG SANDWICH WAFER COOKIES**
- **APPLES, SLICED**
- **PRETZELS**
- **BERRIES**
- **CANDY CORN**

1 Place the Chocolate Hummus in a small bowl. To make the turkey's face, position the Necco Wafers where the eyes should be and then place the M&M'S on top for the pupils.

2 Place the diced Granny Smith apple at the top of the bowl for the turkey's caruncles. Place the Starbursts on a plate, microwave them for 5 seconds, and mold the orange one into a beak shape and the red one into the shape of the wattle. Position them on the hummus.

3 Choose a board, arrange the bowl of hummus at the bottom of it, place the remaining items on the board, and enjoy.

Without a doubt, the traditions are a massive part of what makes Thanksgiving such an important holiday. Between the football, the gathering with family, the turkey, stuffing, and seemingly endless sides, the array of pies and cookies, and the inevitable postdinner naps, it is the standbys that make the day stand out in our minds. But the power of these deeply rooted traditions doesn't mean that you shouldn't try to push the envelope a little bit, and express your creative side. This board does just that, putting a unique spin on the dessert spread while still capturing the spirit of the day.

Chocolate Hummus

Yield: 6 Servings / Active Time: 20 Minutes / Total Time: 1 Hour and 20 Minutes

⅓ cup milk chocolate chips

1 (15 oz.) can of chickpeas, drained and rinsed

⅓ cup unsweetened cocoa powder

¼ cup maple syrup

1 teaspoon pure vanilla extract

½ teaspoon kosher salt

2 tablespoons whole milk or almond milk, plus more as needed

1 Place the chocolate chips in a microwave-safe bowl and microwave for 1 minute. Remove the bowl from the microwave, stir, and then microwave in 15-second intervals until the chocolate chips are almost melted, stirring after each interval. Remove the bowl from the microwave and stir until the chocolate chips are smooth. Set the melted chocolate chips aside and let them cool slightly.

2 In a food processor, add the chickpeas, cocoa powder, syrup, vanilla, and salt and blitz until the mixture is smooth.

3 Transfer the mixture to a mixing bowl, add the melted chocolate, and stir to combine.

4 Gradually add the milk and stir until the hummus has the desired consistency. Chill it in the refrigerator for 1 hour before serving.

Christmas Wreath Board

- SPICED NUTS (SEE PAGE 128)

- PEANUT CLUSTERS (SEE PAGE 129)

- COOL WHIP CANDIES (SEE PAGE 132)

- HOMEMADE TURTLE CANDIES (SEE PAGE 134)

- HOMEMADE PEANUT BUTTER CUPS (SEE PAGE 136)

- COOKIE DOUGH TRUFFLES (SEE PAGE 188)

- NO-BAKE PEANUT BUTTER & CHOCOLATE COOKIES (SEE PAGE 185)

- PRETZEL HUGS (SEE PAGE 70)

- CHOCOLATE CRINKLE COOKIES (SEE PAGE 156)

- CREAM CHEESE MINTS (SEE PAGE 22)

- ASSORTED CANDIES

- CANDY CANES

- PEPPERMINT STICKS

1   Choose a board, arrange all of the items on it in the desired manner, and enjoy.

Grab a round board and your favorite ribbon, it's time to usher in the Christmas season with this festive board, and make sure the entire family is on the same page. Start with some tiny mugs filled with your favorite Christmas-themed candies, and then load up the edge of the board with a stunning variety of homemade treats—a lineup that the Cool Whip Candies and Homemade Turtle Candies serve as the stars of.

Spiced Nuts

Yield: 4 Cups / Active Time: 15 Minutes / Total Time: 1 Hour and 20 Minutes

2 tablespoons unsalted butter

4 teaspoons Worcestershire sauce

3 cups mixed nuts

1 cup whole cashews

1 teaspoon seasoned salt

1   Preheat the oven to 225°F.

2   Line a baking sheet with parchment paper or a silicone mat.

3   Place the butter in a microwave-safe bowl and microwave it until it is melted, about 20 seconds. Remove the butter from the microwave, add the Worcestershire sauce, and stir to combine.

4   Place the mixed nuts and cashews in a large mixing bowl. Add the butter mixture, toss to coat, and spread the nuts on the baking sheet in an even layer.

5   Season the nuts with the salt, place them in the oven, and bake until they are toasted, stirring every 10 minutes.

6   Remove the nuts from the oven and let the nuts cool completely before serving.

Peanut Clusters

Yield: 48 Clusters / Active Time: 35 Minutes / Total Time: 1 Hour and 5 Minutes

1½ lbs. salted roasted peanuts

1¾ cups butterscotch chips

1⅓ cups semisweet chocolate chips

1   Line a large baking sheet with parchment paper. Place the peanuts in a large mixing bowl.

2   Place the butterscotch chips and chocolate chips in a microwave-safe bowl and microwave for 1 minute. Remove the bowl from the microwave, stir, and then microwave the mixture in 15-second intervals until it is almost melted, stirring after each interval. Remove the bowl from the microwave and stir until the mixture is smooth.

3   Pour the chocolate-and-butterscotch mixture over the peanuts and stir to coat.

4   Spoon small piles of the mixture onto the baking sheet and place it in the refrigerator until the clusters are set, about 30 minutes.

5   Remove the clusters from the refrigerator and serve.

Cool Whip Candies

Yield: 36 Candies / Active Time: 30 Minutes / Total Time: 1 Hour and 15 Minutes

1½ lbs. milk chocolate chips   1½ lbs. coating chocolate

1 cup Cool Whip, thawed

1   Line a square 8-inch baking pan with parchment paper.

2   Place the chocolate chips in a microwave-safe bowl and microwave for 1 minute. Remove the bowl from the microwave, stir, and then microwave in 15-second intervals until the chocolate is almost melted, stirring after each interval. Remove the bowl from the microwave and stir the chocolate until smooth.

3   Let the chocolate cool to room temperature, about 15 minutes.

4   Place the Cool Whip in a large mixing bowl, add the melted chocolate, and stir to combine. Spread the mixture in the baking pan, place it in the freezer, and chill for 30 minutes.

5   Line a baking sheet with parchment paper.

6   Remove the baking pan from the freezer and cut the chocolate mixture into small squares.

7   Place the squares on the baking sheet.

8   Break the coating chocolate into squares and place them in a microwave-safe bowl. Microwave for 1 minute. Remove the bowl from the microwave, stir, and then microwave in 15-second intervals until the chocolate is almost melted, stirring after each interval. Remove the bowl from the microwave and stir until the chocolate is smooth.

9   Dip each square into the melted chocolate until completely coated, place them back on the baking sheet, and let the chocolate set before serving. Store the candies in the freezer if not serving immediately.

Homemade Turtle Candies

Yield: 48 Candies / Active Time: 30 Minutes / Total Time: 45 Minutes

1 lb. pecan halves

1 (14 oz.) can of sweetened condensed milk

¾ cup light corn syrup

½ cup sugar

⅓ cup packed brown sugar

¼ cup unsalted butter, cubed

1 teaspoon pure vanilla extract

¾ lb. chocolate melting wafers

Flaky sea salt, for topping (optional)

1   Line a large baking sheet with parchment paper.

2   Arrange the pecans in clusters of 4 to 5.

3   In a small saucepan, combine the milk, corn syrup, and sugars. Fit a candy thermometer to the pan and cook the mixture, stirring frequently, until it reaches 238°F. Remove the pan from heat and stir the butter and vanilla into the caramel.

4   Quickly spoon a small amount of caramel onto each pecan cluster and let the clusters set. Place the chocolate wafers in a microwave-safe bowl and microwave for 1 minute. Remove the bowl from the microwave, stir, and then microwave in 15-second intervals until the chocolate is almost melted, stirring after each interval. Remove the bowl from the microwave and stir the chocolate until it is smooth.

5   Top each cluster with a small spoonful of chocolate and some flaky sea salt (if desired). Chill the candies in the refrigerator until they are set, about 15 minutes. Serve or store in the refrigerator, stacking them and placing a piece of parchment paper in between each layer to prevent them from sticking.

Homemade Peanut Butter Cups

Yield: 35 to 40 Cups / Active Time: 35 Minutes / Total Time: 1 Hour

1 cup creamy peanut butter

1½ tablespoons unsalted butter, softened

½ cup confectioners' sugar

½ teaspoon kosher salt

2 cups chocolate chips

6 oz. chocolate bars

Colored sprinkles, for topping (optional)

1   Line the wells of a mini muffin pan with paper liners. In a small bowl, combine ½ cup of peanut butter, the butter, confectioners' sugar, and salt. Mix until smooth and set it aside.

2   Place the chocolate chips, chocolate bars, and remaining peanut butter in a microwave-safe bowl and microwave for 1 minute. Remove the bowl from the microwave, stir, and then microwave the mixture in 15-second intervals until the chocolate is almost melted, stirring after each interval. Remove the bowl from the microwave and stir the mixture until smooth.

3   Drop 1 to 2 teaspoons of the chocolate mixture into each liner.

4   Top the chocolate mixture with a scant teaspoon of the peanut butter mixture and then cover the peanut butter mixture with more of the chocolate mixture.

5   Top the peanut butter cups with sprinkles (if desired) and chill them in the refrigerator until set.

Christmas Cookie Decorating Board

- **CUT-OUT COOKIES**

- **GINGERBREAD MEN (SEE PAGE 142)**

- **RED, WHITE, AND GREEN FROSTING**

- **ASSORTED CHRISTMAS SPRINKLES AND CANDIES**

1   Choose a board, arrange all of the items on it in the desired manner, and decorate the cookies with your family and friends before enjoying.

Decorating cookies is a holiday tradition for many, but that doesn't mean there's no opportunity to update and improve. This simple board does just that, putting everything right out in front to help everyone envision their ideal design. Store-bought frosting will suffice for decorating the cookies, but I strongly recommend adding some festive food coloring to the Buttercream Frosting on page 25, and filling piping bags with each color.

Gingerbread Board

- **ICED GINGERBREAD MEN (SEE PAGE 142)**

- **GINGERBREAD DIP (SEE PAGE 144)**

- **GINGERSNAPS**

- **NILLA WAFERS**

- **GRAHAM CRACKER STICKS**

1   Choose a board, arrange all of the items on it in the desired manner, and enjoy.

Once you've decorated your Gingerbread Men (see page 142), it's time to show off what you've done. This board lets you do just that, and it leans fully in to the rich sweetness and comforting spice that is gingerbread's trademark, offering the beloved flavor in two different kinds of cookies and an inventive spread.

Iced Gingerbread Men

Yield: 36 to 40 Cookies / Active Time: 35 Minutes / Total Time: 4 Hours

1 To begin preparations for the cookies, place the flour, ginger, cinnamon, baking soda, allspice, and salt in a mixing bowl and whisk to combine. Set the mixture aside.

2 In the work bowl of a stand mixer fitted with the paddle attachment, cream the butter until it is light and fluffy, 4 to 5 minutes.

3 Add the molasses and water and beat to incorporate.

4 With the mixer running, gradually add the dry mixture until the mixture comes together as a smooth dough.

5 Divide the dough in half, form each piece into a disk, and cover them in plastic wrap.

6 Chill the dough in the refrigerator for 2 hours.

7 Preheat the oven to 350°F. Line two baking sheets with parchment paper or silicone mats. Remove 1 disk of the dough from the refrigerator and let it warm up for 10 minutes.

8 Place the dough on a flour-dusted work surface and roll it out to ¼ inch thick.

9 Using cookie cutters, cut the dough into the desired shapes and place them on a baking sheet. Place the cookies in the oven and bake until the edges are set, 12 to 14 minutes. Remove the cookies from the oven, transfer them to a wire rack, and let them cool completely.

10 Repeat Steps 8 and 9 with the other piece of dough.

11 To prepare the icing, place all of the ingredients in a mixing bowl and whisk until smooth. If the frosting is too thick, incorporate more milk.

12 Glaze the cookies with the icing, top them with colored sprinkles, spice drops, and candies, and serve.

For the Cookies

5 cups all-purpose flour, plus more as needed

2 teaspoons ground ginger

2 teaspoons cinnamon

1½ teaspoons baking soda

½ teaspoon allspice

¼ teaspoon kosher salt

1 cup unsalted butter

1 cup molasses

¼ cup water

For the Icing

3 cups sifted confectioners' sugar

2 tablespoons light corn syrup

1 teaspoon clear vanilla extract

2 tablespoons whole milk, plus more as needed

Colored sprinkles, for topping

Spice drops, for topping

Assorted candies, for topping

Gingerbread Dip

½ lb. cream cheese, softened

2 tablespoons brown sugar

2 tablespoons molasses

1½ teaspoons cinnamon

1 teaspoon ground ginger

¼ teaspoon freshly grated nutmeg

1 In the work bowl of a stand mixer fitted with the paddle attachment, beat the cream cheese until it is fluffy, about 3 to 4 minutes.

2 Add the remaining ingredients and beat to incorporate. Transfer the dip to a serving bowl, cover it with plastic wrap, and chill it in the refrigerator for 1 hour before serving.

Reindeer Board

- **RED VELVET CHEESE BALL (SEE PAGE 148)**
- **YOGURT RAISINS, FOR TOPPING**

- **PRETZELS**
- **COOKIES**
- **ASSORTED CANDIES**

1 Using a reindeer-shaped board, remove a large scoop from the cheese ball and place it in the center for the nose.

2 To make the eyes, arrange miniature cupcake liners above the nose to either side and add the yogurt raisins to them.

3 Arrange the remaining items on the board and enjoy.

When I first saw this reindeer-themed serving board (I found mine at World Market, but they should be available at any holiday store, and at home stores around the holidays), I just had to have it. I knew that there would be no shortage of uses for it as Christmas approached, but this board is one of the best that I have found so far. Spend a little bit of time in the afternoon getting the Red Velvet Cheese Ball ready, queue up *Rudolph the Red-Nosed Reindeer* in the evening, and soak up the joy of the season.

Red Velvet Cheese Ball

Yield: 10 to 12 Servings / Active Time: 30 Minutes / Total Time: 3 Hours and 30 Minutes

½ lb. cream cheese, softened

½ cup unsalted butter, softened

1¾ cups red velvet cake mix

1 cup confectioners' sugar

2 tablespoons brown sugar

Miniature chocolate chips, for coating (optional)

Chocolate sprinkles, for coating (optional)

1 In the work bowl of a stand mixer fitted with the paddle attachment, beat the cream cheese until it is fluffy, about 5 minutes.

2 Add the butter and beat until the mixture is light and fluffy.

3 Add the cake mix, confectioners' sugar, and brown sugar and beat until thoroughly combined.

4 Using plastic wrap, form the mixture into a ball and chill it in the refrigerator for 1 hour.

5 Place chocolate chips or chocolate sprinkles on a plate and roll the cheese ball in them until it is completely coated. Chill the cheese ball in the refrigerator for 2 hours before serving.

Christmas Board

- **EGGNOG DIP (SEE PAGE 152)**

- **SALTINE TOFFEE (SEE PAGE 154)**

- **CHOCOLATE CRINKLE COOKIES (SEE PAGE 156)**

- **OREO BALLS (SEE PAGE 71)**

- **ICED GINGERBREAD MEN (SEE PAGE 142)**

- **PEANUT BUTTER BLOSSOMS (SEE PAGE 186)**

- **JAM CAKES (SEE PAGE 184)**

- **NO-BAKE PEANUT BUTTER & CHOCOLATE COOKIES (SEE PAGE 185)**

- **CHOCOLATE CHIP COOKIES (SEE PAGE 182)**

- **HOMEMADE PEANUT BUTTER CUPS (SEE PAGE 136)**

- **PRETZEL HUGS (SEE PAGE 70)**

- **ASSORTED CHRISTMAS CANDIES**

- **CANDY CANES**

1 Choose a board, arrange all of the items on it in the desired manner, and enjoy.

When the big day arrives, you want to make sure that you have a spread that surpasses expectations, and contains everyone's favorite treats. This board does just that for my family—make sure you swap in whatever confections are loved by your loved ones. And, if you are one of those who throw a big Christmas party every year, consider arranging a few of these around the house so that people can graze as they mingle.

Eggnog Dip

Yield: 8 to 10 Servings / Active Time: 30 Minutes / Total Time: 1 Hour and 30 Minutes

½ lb. cream cheese, softened

½ cup eggnog

½ teaspoon rum extract

½ teaspoon pure vanilla extract

½ teaspoon cinnamon

¼ teaspoon freshly grated nutmeg

2 cups confectioners' sugar

1 cup Cool Whip, thawed

Cookies or graham crackers, for serving

Fruit, for serving

1 In the work bowl of a stand mixer fitted with the paddle attachment, beat the cream cheese until it is light and fluffy.

2 Add the eggnog, rum extract, vanilla, cinnamon, and nutmeg and beat until the mixture is smooth.

3 Add the confectioners' sugar in three to four increments, beating to incorporate each one before adding the next.

4 Add the Cool Whip and fold to incorporate. Transfer the dip to a clean bowl and chill it in the refrigerator for 1 hour before serving with cookies or graham crackers and fruit.

Saltine Toffee

Yield: 20 Pieces / Active Time: 35 Minutes / Total Time: 2 Hours and 15 Minutes

40 saltines

1 cup unsalted butter, cubed

1 cup brown sugar

¾ lb. chocolate chips or chocolate melting wafers

1 cup English toffee pieces

½ cup chopped pecans

1 Preheat the oven to 350°F. Line a 15 x 10–inch rimmed baking sheet with aluminum foil. Arrange the saltines on the baking sheet in a single layer. In a heavy saucepan, melt the butter. Stir in the brown sugar and bring the mixture to a boil. Cook, stirring continually, until the sugar has dissolved, 1 to 2 minutes.

2 Pour the mixture evenly over the crackers.

3 Place the baking sheet in the oven and bake until the topping is bubbly, about 6 minutes.

4 While the saltines are in the oven, place the chocolate in a microwave-safe bowl and microwave for 1 minute. Remove the bowl from the microwave, stir, and then microwave in 15-second intervals until the chocolate is almost melted, stirring after each interval. Remove the chocolate from the microwave and stir until it is smooth.

5 Remove the baking sheet from the oven and carefully spread the melted chocolate over the mixture.

6 Sprinkle the toffee and pecans over the chocolate and let the saltine toffee cool completely.

7 Cover the saltine toffee with plastic wrap and chill it in the refrigerator until set, about 1 hour.

8 Break the toffee into pieces and serve.

Chocolate Crinkle Cookies

Yield: 48 Cookies / Active Time: 35 Minutes / Total Time: 24 Hours

1 In a small bowl, whisk together the flour, baking powder, and salt. Set the mixture aside.

2 Place the chocolate in a microwave-safe bowl and microwave for 1 minute. Remove the bowl from the microwave, stir, and then microwave in 15-second intervals until the chocolate is almost melted, stirring after each interval. Remove the chocolate from the microwave and stir until it is smooth.

3 In the work bowl of a stand mixer fitted with the paddle attachment, beat the canola oil, sugar, and melted chocolate until well combined.

4 Incorporate the eggs one at a time, add the vanilla, and beat to incorporate.

5 With the mixer running, gradually add the dry mixture and beat until the mixture comes together as a smooth dough. Transfer the dough to a clean bowl, cover it tightly with plastic wrap, and chill the dough in the refrigerator overnight.

6 Preheat the oven to 350°F.

7 Line baking sheets with parchment paper or silicone baking mats.

8 Place the confectioners' sugar in a shallow bowl. Remove the dough from the refrigerator, form it into balls, and roll them in the confectioners' sugar until they are completely coated.

9 Place the cookies on the baking sheets, place them in the oven, and bake until they are set around the edges, 8 to 10 minutes. Remove the cookies from the oven and let them cool completely before serving.

2 cups all-purpose flour

2 teaspoons baking powder

½ teaspoon kosher salt

2 oz. Baker's Chocolate

½ cup canola oil

2 cups sugar

4 large eggs, at room temperature

2 teaspoons pure vanilla extract

1 cup confectioners' sugar

Hot Cocoa Board

- **PEPPERMINT CANDIES, CRUSHED, FOR TOPPING**

- **1½ LBS. COATING CHOCOLATE**

- **MARSHMALLOWS, SOME DICED, SOME LEFT WHOLE**

- **HOT CHOCOLATE BOMBS (SEE PAGE 160)**

- **CHOCOLATE MACARONS**

- **CHOCOLATE CANDIES**

1 Line a baking sheet with parchment paper. Place the crushed peppermint candies in a bowl.

2 Place the coating chocolate in a microwave-safe bowl and microwave for 1 minute. Remove the bowl from the microwave, stir, and then microwave in 15-second intervals until the chocolate is almost melted, stirring after each interval. Remove the bowl from the microwave and stir until the chocolate is smooth.

3 Dip the bowls of wooden spoons into the melted chocolate and crushed peppermint candies until coated. Place them on the baking sheets and let the melted chocolate set.

4 Dip stirring sticks into the melted chocolate and let the chocolate harden. Repeat two more times. When the final layer has been applied, affix the diced marshmallows to the chocolate and let the chocolate set.

5 Choose a board, arrange the coated spoons, stirring sticks, and other items on it in the desired manner, and enjoy.

When the winter weather gets truly frightening, fix up this board and curl up by the fire. With the Hot Chocolate Bombs, chocolate and peppermint–coated spoons, and marshmallow-spiked stirring sticks, an unforgettable cup of cocoa is guaranteed, and the inclusion of a few macarons adds a bit of elegance, highlighting how fortunate everyone is to be safe and warm instead of stuck outside in the wind and snow.

Hot Chocolate Bombs

Yield: 6 to 8 Servings / Active Time: 35 Minutes / Total Time: 45 Minutes

1   Break the coating chocolate into squares, place them in a microwave-safe bowl, and microwave for 1 minute. Remove the bowl from the microwave, stir, and then microwave in 15-second intervals until the chocolate is almost melted, stirring after each interval. Remove the chocolate from the microwave and stir until it is smooth.

2   Spoon small amounts of the melted chocolate into silicone dome molds.

3   Using a paintbrush or the back of the spoon, spread the chocolate evenly around the molds, making sure to get all the way up the sides of the molds.

4   Let the chocolate harden and then repeat until you have 4 layers of chocolate.

5   After applying the final layer, let the shells harden for 5 minutes and then gently remove them from the molds.

6   Warm a microwave-safe plate in the microwave for 15 seconds. Place half of the chocolate shells, open side down, on the plate and let their rims melt a little.

7   Remove the shells from the plate and fill them with some of the hot chocolate mix and mini marshmallows.

8   Warm a clean microwave-safe plate in the microwave for 15 seconds. Place the remaining chocolate shells, open side down, on the plate and let their rims melt a little.

9   Working quickly, place the two open ends of the chocolate shells together and smooth over the seams. Melt the chocolate wafers in the microwave and coat the hot chocolate bombs with them. Top with sprinkles and crushed peppermint candies and place them in mugs. To serve, add warm milk to each mug and stir.

1½ lbs. coating chocolate

2 tablespoons hot chocolate mix

Miniature marshmallows,
as needed

Colored chocolate melting wafers,
for coating

Colored sprinkles, for topping

Peppermint candies, crushed,
for topping

Milk, warmed, for serving

New Year's Eve Board

- **1 CAKE, DECORATED WITH CLOCK HANDS AND COLORED SPRINKLES**

- **CHOCOLATE TRUFFLES (SEE PAGE 206)**

- **CHOCOLATE CUPCAKES (SEE PAGE 98)**

- **WHITE CHOCOLATE–DIPPED FRUIT (STRAWBERRIES AND CHERRIES)**

- **ASSORTED CHOCOLATE CANDIES**

- **CHOCOLATE COINS**

1 Choose a board, arrange all of the items on it in the desired manner, and enjoy.

The arrival of another year is always worth celebrating—make sure you ring it in right with this eye-catching spread! Whether you are heading to a party or hosting at home, the nice thing about this board is that it is easy to put together, which is a must after the all-out sprint the holiday season demands. Really, all you have to do is head to a local craft store for the clock hands. After that, everything you need to put this board together is either easy to procure or already at home.

Super Bowl Board

- SUPER BOWL BARK (SEE PAGE 166)

- HOMEMADE PEANUT BUTTER CUPS (SEE PAGE 136)

- SNICKERDOODLES (SEE PAGE 262)

- FOOTBALL-THEMED COOKIES

- CHOCOLATE CUPCAKES (SEE PAGE 98), DECORATED WITH CHOCOLATE FROSTING

- CHOCOLATE CUPCAKES, DECORATED WITH GREEN FROSTING TO RESEMBLE GRASS

- CHOCOLATE FOOTBALL-SHAPED CANDIES

- SNACK MIX

- SPICED NUTS (SEE PAGE 128)

1   Choose a board, arrange all of the items on it in the desired manner, and enjoy.

Are you ready for some football? Once a year, everyone comes together to stuff their faces, watch the big game, judge the commercials, and criticize the halftime show. This board puts all your ducks in a row when the Super Bowl rolls around, ensuring that even if the game ends up being a dud—which happens more often than not—everyone will still enjoy themselves, stuffing their faces with this collection of sweet and salty snacks.

Super Bowl Bark

Yield: 10 Servings / Active Time: 10 Minutes / Total Time: 35 Minutes

1½ lbs. coating chocolate

Pretzels, broken into pieces, for topping

Colored sprinkles, for topping

1   Line a large baking sheet with parchment paper. Break the coating chocolate into squares and place them in a microwave-safe bowl. Microwave for 1 minute. Remove the bowl from the microwave, stir, and then microwave in 15-second intervals until the chocolate is almost melted, stirring after each interval. Remove the bowl from the microwave and stir until the chocolate is smooth.

2   Pour the chocolate into the baking sheet and spread it with an offset spatula, making sure that it is even.

3   Distribute the pretzels and sprinkles over the chocolate. Let the chocolate sit until it has set, about 20 minutes.

4   Break the chocolate bark into pieces and serve immediately or store in an airtight container.

St. Patrick's Day Board

- **WHOOPIE PIES (SEE PAGE 260), FILLED WITH MINT ICE CREAM**

- **MINT BROWNIE BITES**

- **LUCKY SNACK MIX**

- **MINT CHOCOLATE MIX**

- **GREEN MATCHA POCKY**

- **ANDES MINTS**

- **CHOCOLATE COINS**

- **ROLOS**

1   Choose a board, arrange all of the items on it in the desired manner, and enjoy.

The luck of the Irish is sure to be with you and your crew once you curate this St. Patrick's Day Board. Punctuated with brilliant pops of green and featuring a number of refreshing flavors between the mint and the matcha, this spread is certain to keep the festivities going strong. For the lucky snack mix, I like to add green mint chocolate candies to a savory Chex Mix, but feel free to incorporate them into your go-to mix.

St. Patrick's Day Board, *see page 167*

Valentine Board

- **BAKED DOUGHNUTS (SEE PAGE 171), SOME MINIATURE, SOME HEART SHAPED**

- **CHOCOLATE-DIPPED PRETZEL RODS**

- **CHOCOLATE-DIPPED STRAWBERRIES**

- **STRAWBERRY YOGURT–COATED PRETZELS**

- **LITTLE DEBBIE BE MY VALENTINE SNACK CAKES**

- **CANDY CONVERSATION HEARTS**

- **HEART-SHAPED PEANUT BUTTER CUPS**

- **MILK CHOCOLATE BALLS**

- **CHERRY-FLAVORED GUMMY CANDIES**

- **GOOD & PLENTY**

- **CHOCOLATE NECCO WAFERS**

- **HEART-SHAPED GUMMY CANDIES**

- **MINIATURE DARK CHOCOLATE CANDY BARS**

- **MILK CHOCOLATE SQUARES**

- **ANIMAL CRACKERS (CHOCOLATE AND TRADITIONAL)**

1 Choose a board, arrange the items on it in the desired manner, and enjoy.

Spread the love this Valentine's Day with a board that is freighted with heart-shaped baked goods, decadent bites, and romantic reds and pinks. This spread is great whether you and your special someone decide to save some dough and celebrate at home, or if you and a group of friends are going solo and hanging together for solidarity.

Baked Doughnuts

Yield: 12 to 24 Doughnuts / Active Time: 25 Minutes / Total Time: 1 Hour and 20 Minutes

1 (15¼ oz.) box of cake mix

2 large eggs, at room temperature

½ cup unsalted butter, softened

1 cup whole milk

Vanilla Glaze (see page 228)

1 Preheat the oven to 350°F.

2 Coat two doughnut pans with nonstick cooking spray.

3 In a large bowl, beat the cake mix, eggs, butter, and milk until the mixture comes together as a smooth batter.

4 Spoon the batter into the wells of the doughnut pans, filling each well about halfway.

5 Place the doughnuts in the oven and bake until they are golden brown and a toothpick inserted into their centers comes out clean, 7 to 10 minutes. The baking time will depend on the sizes of the doughnuts.

6 Remove the doughnuts from the oven and briefly let them cool in the pans. Transfer the doughnuts to a wire rack and let them cool completely before applying the glaze and serving.

Valentine Board, see page 170

Winter Board

- **VANILLA CUPCAKES (SEE PAGE 218), FROSTED AND DECORATED WITH SPRINKLES**

- **WINTER OREO BALLS (SEE PAGE 177)**

- **MARSHMALLOW SNOWMEN (SEE PAGE 176)**

- **WHITE CHOCOLATE–DIPPED GRAHAM CRACKERS**

- **ASSORTED BLUE AND WHITE CANDIES**

- **MINIATURE MARSHMALLOWS**

- **YOGURT RAISINS**

1 Choose a board, arrange the items on it in the desired manner, and enjoy.

Does a big storm have you in the mood to build a snowman or test out your toboggan at the nearest sledding hill? Prepare this board before heading out, and you'll be able to have a blast in the winter wonderland, knowing that you can cozy up with this spread when you're done. The key here is leaning completely in to the monochromatic look, punctuating the almost-complete whiteout only occasionally.

Marshmallow Snowmen

Yield: 6 Servings / Active Time: 20 Minutes / Total Time: 20 Minutes

18 marshmallows

6 Tootsie Rolls

¼ cup chocolate melting wafers

6 Rolos

Colored candy balls, as needed

8 pretzel sticks

Confectioners' sugar, for topping

1 Take six skewers and thread three marshmallows onto each one. Set the marshmallows aside.

2 Place the Tootsie Rolls on a plate and microwave them for 5 seconds. Remove them from the microwave and press down until they are flat disks.

3 Place the chocolate wafers in a microwave-safe bowl and microwave for 1 minute. Remove the bowl from the microwave, stir, and then microwave in 15-second intervals until the chocolate is almost melted, stirring after each interval. Remove the chocolate from the microwave and stir until smooth.

4 Spread some melted chocolate on top of the flattened Tootsie Rolls and then affix a Rolo on top of each one so that they resemble hats.

5 Spread some melted chocolate on top of the top marshmallow on each skewer and affix the hats to them. Dot the top and middle marshmallows with some melted chocolate and affix the colored candy balls to them to make eyes, mouths, and buttons.

6 Break 2 of the pretzel sticks into thirds and the remaining pretzel sticks in half. Stick the smaller pieces into the top marshmallows to make noses, and the larger pieces into the sides of middle marshmallows to make arms.

7 Dust the snowmen with confectioners' sugar and serve.

Winter Oreo Balls

Yield: 28 Balls / Active Time: 40 Minutes / Total Time: 4 Hours and 15 Minutes

1 (20 oz.) package of Oreos

½ lb. cream cheese, softened

1 lb. vanilla-flavored coating chocolate

Colored sprinkles, for topping

1 Line a baking sheet with parchment paper. Place the Oreos in a food processor and pulse until they are crushed. Add half of the cream cheese, pulse to incorporate, and then add the remaining cream cheese. Pulse to incorporate, making sure that the mixture is well combined enough to form it into balls.

2 Form the mixture into balls, place them on the baking sheet, and chill them in the refrigerator for 3 hours.

3 Line a large baking sheet with parchment paper. Break the coating chocolate into squares and place them in a microwave-safe bowl. Microwave for 1 minute. Remove the bowl from the microwave, stir, and then microwave in 15-second intervals until the chocolate is almost melted, stirring after each interval. Remove the bowl from the microwave and stir until the chocolate is smooth.

4 Remove 4 to 6 balls from the refrigerator at a time. Secure the balls with two forks and dip them into the melted chocolate until they are completely coated. Use the sprinkles to make a snowman face on each ball and let the chocolate set for 15 minutes before serving or storing in the refrigerator.

FALL & WINTER

177

Boards for All Seasons

Sure, building a dessert board around a holiday or a certain seasonal flavor or item makes a lot of sense. But there are plenty of moments throughout the year when a curated collection of confections can transform a day into something unforgettable. Maybe it's a loved one's birthday. Maybe you want to push your child's first sleepover over the top. Or maybe you just want to make movie night feel a little more special. These, and many more moments, cry out for just a little creativity and a little sweetness—luckily, those are your specialties.

Any Occasion Board

- **CHOCOLATE CRINKLE COOKIES (SEE PAGE 156)**

- **CHOCOLATE CHIP COOKIES (SEE PAGE 182)**

- **JAM CAKES (SEE PAGE 184)**

- **SNICKERDOODLES (SEE PAGE 262)**

- **NO-BAKE PEANUT BUTTER & CHOCOLATE COOKIES (SEE PAGE 185)**

- **PEANUT BUTTER BLOSSOMS (SEE PAGE 186)**

- **COOKIE DOUGH TRUFFLES (SEE PAGE 188)**

- **HOMEMADE PEANUT BUTTER CUPS (SEE PAGE 136)**

- **SPICED NUTS (SEE PAGE 128)**

- **STRAWBERRIES**

1 Choose a board, arrange all of the items on it in the desired manner, and enjoy.

For my family, this board is the go-to, featuring recipes passed down from my sister (Chocolate Crinkle Cookies) and mother-in-law (Jam Cakes and No-Bake Peanut Butter & Chocolate Cookies), and the rest of the clan's favorite treats. No doubt, this board will take on a different look depending on your own family's beloved bites—the most important thing is having a board that you can turn to when some comfort is what's called for.

Chocolate Chip Cookies

Yield: 48 Cookies / Active Time: 30 Minutes / Total Time: 1 Hour and 30 Minutes

2 cups all-purpose flour

1 teaspoon kosher salt

¾ teaspoon baking soda

¾ cup unsalted butter, softened

1¼ cups packed brown sugar

2 tablespoons whole milk

1 tablespoon pure vanilla extract

1 large egg, at room temperature

1 cup chocolate chips

1 Preheat the oven to 350°F. Line multiple baking sheets with parchment paper or silicone mats. In a small bowl, whisk together the flour, salt, and baking soda. Set the mixture aside.

2 In the work bowl of a stand mixer fitted with the paddle attachment, beat the butter and brown sugar until fluffy.

3 Add the milk and vanilla and beat to incorporate. Add the egg and beat to incorporate.

4 With the mixer running, gradually add the flour mixture and beat until the mixture just comes together as a smooth dough, making sure not to overmix. Add the chocolate chips and beat until they are evenly distributed.

5 Form the dough into balls and place them on the baking sheets.

6 Place the cookies in the oven and bake until they are golden brown around the edges and still a little soft in the center, 10 to 12 minutes.

7 Remove the cookies from the oven and let the cookies cool on the baking sheets for 2 minutes before transferring them to a wire rack to cool completely.

Jam Cakes

Yield: 2 Large or 6 Small Cakes / Active Time: 30 Minutes / Total Time: 1 Hour and 35 Minutes

4 cups all-purpose flour, plus more as needed

2 teaspoons baking soda

2 teaspoons cinnamon

1 teaspoon allspice

1 teaspoon freshly grated nutmeg

⅛ teaspoon kosher salt

2 cups sugar

½ cup canola oil

2 cups buttermilk

1 cup strawberry jam

1 cup raisins

½ cup chopped nuts (walnuts or pecans)

1 Preheat the oven to 375°F. Coat your loaf pans with nonstick cooking spray and dust them with flour, knocking out any excess.

2 In a medium bowl, whisk together the flour, baking soda, spices, and salt. Set the mixture aside.

3 In the work bowl of a stand mixer fitted with the paddle attachment, beat the sugar and canola oil until the mixture is fluffy, about 3 minutes. Add the buttermilk and beat to incorporate. Add the jam and beat to incorporate.

4 Set 2 tablespoons of the dry mixture aside. With the mixer running, gradually add the remaining dry mixture to the wet mixture until the mixture comes together as a smooth dough.

5 Place the raisins in a small bowl, add the reserved dry mixture, and toss to coat. Add them to the batter and beat until they are evenly distributed. Add the nuts and beat until they are evenly distributed.

6 Divide the mixture among the loaf pans. Place the pans in the oven and bake the cakes until a toothpick inserted in their centers comes out clean, 40 to 50 minutes. Remove the cakes from the oven and let them cool in the pans for 10 to 15 minutes. Remove the cakes from the pans and let them to cool completely on a wire rack before serving.

No-Bake Peanut Butter & Chocolate Cookies

Yield: 36 Cookies / Active Time: 25 Minutes / Total Time: 1 Hour and 30 Minutes

3 cups quick-cooking oats

½ cup creamy peanut butter

2 cups sugar

⅓ cup unsweetened cocoa powder

½ cup milk

½ cup unsalted butter

2 teaspoons pure vanilla extract

1   Line two baking sheets with parchment paper and set out a couple of spoons. Place the oats in a large bowl.

2   Measure the peanut butter and set it aside.

3   In a small saucepan, whisk together the sugar and cocoa powder.

4   Add the milk and butter and stir to combine.

5   Warm the mixture over medium heat, stirring continually.

6   When the mixture begins to simmer, set a timer for 2 minutes.

7   Continue to stir until the timer goes off.

8   Remove the pan from heat and pour the mixture over the oats.

9   Stir the mixture slightly, add the peanut butter and vanilla, and stir until the mixture is thoroughly combined. Working quickly, spoon the cookies onto the baking sheets.

10 Let the cookies cool completely and set before serving.

Peanut Butter Blossoms

Yield: 36 to 40 Cookies / Active Time: 30 Minutes / Total Time: 2 Hours and 30 Minutes

1 In a small bowl, whisk together the flour, salt, and baking soda. Set the mixture aside.

2 In the work bowl of a stand mixer fitted with the paddle attachment, cream the peanut butter, butter, and brown sugar until the mixture is fluffy, 4 to 5 minutes. Add the milk and vanilla and beat to incorporate. Add the egg and beat to incorporate.

3 With the mixer running, gradually add the flour mixture until the mixture comes together as a smooth dough.

4 Transfer the dough to a clean bowl and cover it with plastic wrap. Chill the dough in the refrigerator for 1 hour. The dough will keep in the refrigerator overnight.

5 Preheat the oven to 350°F.

6 Line two baking sheets with parchment paper or silicone mats. Unwrap the chocolate kisses and place the sugar in a small bowl.

7 Form the dough into balls and then roll the balls in the sugar.

8 Place the balls on the baking sheets, place them in the oven, and bake until the cookies are light brown around the edges and just set in their centers, 8 to 10 minutes.

9 Remove the cookies from the oven and immediately place a chocolate kiss in the center of each cookie, gently pressing down.

10 Transfer the cookies to a wire rack and let them cool completely before serving.

1¾ cups all-purpose flour

¾ teaspoon kosher salt

¾ teaspoon baking soda

¾ cup creamy peanut butter

½ cup unsalted butter, softened

1¼ cups packed brown sugar

3 tablespoons whole milk

1 tablespoon pure vanilla extract

1 large egg, at room temperature

40 chocolate kisses

Sugar, for coating

Cookie Dough Truffles

Yield: 40 to 45 Truffles / Active Time: 35 Minutes / Total Time: 3 Hours and 5 Minutes

1   In the work bowl of a stand mixer fitted with the paddle attachment, cream together the butter and brown sugar until the mixture is fluffy, 4 to 5 minutes.

2   Add the vanilla and beat to incorporate.

3   With the mixer running, gradually add the flour and milk, alternating between them. Add the chocolate chips and beat until they are evenly distributed.

4   Transfer the dough to a clean bowl and chill it in the freezer for about 1 hour.

5   Remove the dough from the freezer.

6   Line baking sheets with parchment paper. Form the dough into balls and place them on the baking sheets. Chill the balls in the freezer for 30 minutes to 1 hour.

7   Place the coating chocolate in a microwave-safe bowl and heat it in the microwave for 1 minute. Remove the chocolate from the microwave, stir it, and continue heating it in 30-second intervals until the chocolate is almost melted. Remove the chocolate from the microwave and stir until it is completely smooth.

8   Line another baking sheet with parchment paper.

9   Remove 5 to 6 balls from the freezer, and, using a fork and knife, dip the balls into the melted chocolate until they are completely coated, allowing any excess to drip off into the bowl.

10 Place the truffles on the baking sheet and top them with sprinkles and candy melts.

11 Repeat with the remaining balls of dough.

12 Let the truffles sit for 15 to 30 minutes before serving. Store in the refrigerator.

- ½ cup unsalted butter, melted

- ¾ cup packed brown sugar

- 1 teaspoon vanilla extract

- 2 cups all-purpose flour

- 1 (14 oz.) can of sweetened condensed milk

- ½ cup miniature chocolate chips

- 1½ lbs. coating chocolate (vanilla flavored or milk chocolate)

- Sprinkles, for topping

- Colored candy melts, for topping

Note: If you prefer not to work with raw flour, preheat the oven to 325°F. Evenly spread the flour on a large baking sheet. Place the flour in the oven and bake until it is 160°F, about 7 minutes. Remove the flour from the oven and let it cool completely before using.

Popcorn Board

- **CAKE BATTER POPCORN (SEE PAGE 192)**

- **NUTTY CHOCOLATE & CARAMEL POPCORN (SEE PAGE 194)**

- **CHEDDAR & CARAMEL POPCORN**

- **POPCORN, POPPED, WITH WHITE CHOCOLATE DRIZZLED OVER IT AND SPRINKLES**

- **KETTLE CORN, WITH PRETZELS AND POTATO CHIPS MIXED IN**

1 Choose a board, arrange all of the items on it in the desired manner, and enjoy.

Perfect for a movie night or a sleepover, this board is a great one to break out on those nights when everyone is getting cozy. It also operates on a good guiding principle—find a way to make something store-bought seem a bit more special. You'll turn to this concept time and again once you move past this collection of boards and start coming up with your own, as it allows you to cut down on your workload while still transforming the evening into an occasion.

Cake Batter Popcorn

Yield: 8 Cups / Active Time: 15 Minutes / Total Time: 30 Minutes

8 cups popped plain popcorn

1 lb. vanilla-flavored coating chocolate

½ cup dry cake mix

½ cup rainbow sprinkles

1 Line a large baking sheet with parchment paper. Place the popcorn in a large bowl and set it aside.

2 Place the coating chocolate in a microwave-safe bowl and microwave for 1 minute. Remove the bowl from the microwave, stir, and then microwave in 15-second intervals until the chocolate is almost melted, stirring after each interval. Remove the chocolate from the microwave and stir until it is smooth.

3 Stir the cake mix into the melted chocolate until combined.

4 Pour the melted chocolate mixture over the popcorn and toss to coat.

5 Spread the popcorn on the baking sheet, top with the sprinkles, and let the chocolate set for 15 to 20 minutes.

6 Break the popcorn into small pieces and serve.

Nutty Chocolate & Caramel Popcorn

Yield: 10 Cups / Active Time: 15 Minutes / Total Time: 35 Minutes

8 cups popped plain popcorn

1 cup chopped pecans

1 cup chopped walnuts

1 cup chocolate chips

Caramel Sauce (see page 89), warm

1 Line a baking sheet with aluminum foil.

2 Place the popcorn in a large bowl, add the nuts, and toss to combine. Set the mixture aside.

3 Place the chocolate chips in a microwave-safe bowl and microwave for 1 minute. Remove the bowl from the microwave, stir, and then microwave in 15-second intervals until the chocolate chips are almost melted, stirring after each interval. Remove the bowl from the microwave and stir until the chocolate chips are smooth. Set the melted chocolate chips aside.

4 Pour the caramel over the popcorn mixture and stir to coat. Drizzle the melted chocolate over the popcorn mixture and spread in an even layer on the baking sheet. Let the caramel and chocolate set for 20 minutes.

5 Break the popcorn mixture into small pieces and serve.

Birthday Board

- **FUNFETTI SHORTBREAD (SEE PAGE 198)**

- **FROSTED SUGAR COOKIES (SEE PAGE 200 FOR HOMEMADE)**

- **FUNFETTI CUPCAKES**

- **ICE CREAM**

- **CAKE MIX COOKIES (SEE PAGE 107), MADE WITH FUNFETTI CAKE MIX**

- **CLASSIC CHOCOLATE BARK (SEE PAGE 202)**

- **ASSORTED COLORED CANDIES**

1 Choose a board, arrange all of the items on it in the desired manner, and enjoy.

Whether you've got a big crew coming together to celebrate or you're just looking to make sure that someone's special day feels that way, this board has everything you need—from classic festive treats like cupcakes, ice cream, and chocolate bark to moist and crumbly Cake Mix Cookies, a recipe that is invaluable to the dessert board devotee, as it is easy to prepare, and incredibly versatile.

Funfetti Shortbread

Yield: 12 Servings / Active Time: 30 Minutes / Total Time: 2 Hours and 40 Minutes

1 In the work bowl of a stand mixer fitted with the paddle attachment, beat the butter and sugar until the mixture is fluffy, about 5 minutes.

2 Add the egg and beat to incorporate. Gradually add the flour and beat until the mixture comes together as a smooth dough. Add the sprinkles and beat until they are evenly distributed.

3 Form the dough into a disk and cover it with plastic wrap.

4 Chill the dough in the refrigerator for 1 hour.

5 Preheat the oven to 375°F. Line a baking sheet with parchment paper or a silicone mat.

6 Place the dough on the baking sheet and roll it into a 12 x 8–inch rectangle.

7 Cut the dough into smaller rectangles.

8 Place the shortbread in the oven and bake until it is golden brown around the edges, 8 to 10 minutes.

9 Remove the shortbread from the oven and let it cool completely.

10 Place the chocolate wafers in a small microwave-safe bowl and microwave for 30 seconds. Remove the bowl, stir the chocolate, and microwave in 15-second intervals until the chocolate is almost melted, stirring after each interval.

11 Remove the bowl from the microwave and stir the chocolate until it is smooth.

12 Transfer the chocolate to a piping bag and snip off the end.

13 Drizzle the chocolate over the shortbread, top it with additional sprinkles, and serve.

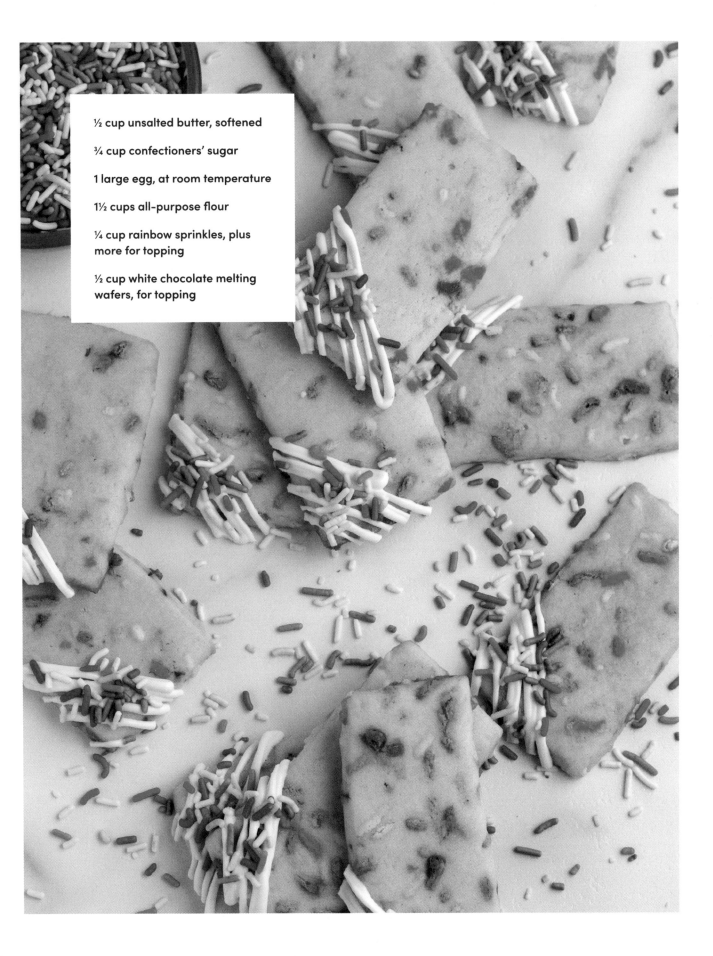

½ cup unsalted butter, softened

¾ cup confectioners' sugar

1 large egg, at room temperature

1½ cups all-purpose flour

¼ cup rainbow sprinkles, plus more for topping

½ cup white chocolate melting wafers, for topping

Frosted Sugar Cookies

Yield: 48 Cookies / Active Time: 30 Minutes / Total Time: 1 Hour and 30 Minutes

1   To begin preparations for the cookies, preheat the oven to 350°F.

2   Line two baking sheets with parchment paper or silicone mats.

3   In a large bowl, whisk together the flour, baking powder, baking soda, and salt. Set the mixture aside.

4   In the work bowl of a stand mixer fitted with the paddle attachment, cream together the butter, sour cream, and sugar until the mixture is light and fluffy. Add the eggs and vanilla and beat to incorporate.

5   With the mixer running, gradually add the dry mixture until the mixture is a smooth dough, scraping down the work bowl as necessary.

6   Form the dough into 2-inch balls and place them on the baking sheets. Wet the bottom of a glass and press down on the balls to flatten them slightly.

7   Place the cookies in the oven and bake until they have puffed up slightly, their edges are set, and their bottoms are lightly browned, 8 to 10 minutes.

8   Remove the cookies from the oven, transfer them to a wire rack, and let them cool completely.

9   To begin preparations for the frosting, place the butter in the work bowl of a stand mixer fitted with the paddle attachment and cream until it is fluffy and smooth.

10 With the mixer running, gradually add the confectioners' sugar and cream, alternating between them. Add more cream if necessary to achieve the desired consistency. Add the vanilla and food coloring (if using) and beat to incorporate.

11 Frost the cookies, decorate them with sprinkles, and serve.

For the Cookies

6 cups all-purpose flour

2 teaspoons baking powder

1 teaspoon baking soda

½ teaspoon kosher salt

1 cup unsalted butter, softened

1 cup sour cream

2 cups sugar

2 large eggs, at room temperature

2 teaspoons pure vanilla extract

For the Frosting

½ cup unsalted butter, softened

2 cups confectioners' sugar

1½ teaspoons heavy whipping cream, plus more as needed

½ teaspoon pure vanilla extract

2 to 3 drops of food coloring (optional)

Colored sprinkles, for decorating

Classic Chocolate Bark

Yield: 10 Servings / Active Time: 10 Minutes / Total Time: 35 Minutes

1½ lbs. vanilla-flavored coating chocolate

Assorted candies (miniature gummy worms, Skittles, Mike and Ike, Nerds, etc.), for topping

Colored sprinkles, for topping

1 Line a large baking sheet with parchment paper. Break the coating chocolate into squares and place them in a microwave-safe bowl. Microwave for 1 minute. Remove the bowl from the microwave, stir, and then microwave in 15-second intervals until the chocolate is almost melted, stirring after each interval. Remove the bowl from the microwave and stir until the chocolate is smooth.

2 Pour the chocolate into the baking sheet and spread it with an offset spatula, making sure that it is even.

3 Distribute the candy and sprinkles over the chocolate and let the chocolate sit until it has set, about 20 minutes.

4 Break the chocolate bark into pieces and serve immediately or store in an airtight container.

Chocolate Lovers Board

- **CHOCOLATE TRUFFLES (SEE PAGE 206)**
- **ASSORTED HIGH-END CHOCOLATES**
- **CHOCOLATE MACARONS**
- **MEXICAN CHOCOLATE COOKIES**

1   Choose a board, arrange all of the items on it in the desired manner, and enjoy.

You don't have to break the bank for this board, but you should be prepared to splurge a little bit, as the difference between midlevel and high-quality chocolate, while always significant, will prove to be particularly glaring on this board. Do that, and you're sure to entrance the chocolate lover in your life.

Chocolate Lovers Board, see page 203

Chocolate Truffles

Yield: 30 Truffles / Active Time: 30 Minutes / Total Time: 5 Hours

3 cups semisweet chocolate chips

1 (14 oz.) can of sweetened condensed milk

1 tablespoon unsalted butter

2 teaspoons pure vanilla extract

Confectioners' sugar, for coating (optional)

Unsweetened cocoa powder, for coating (optional)

Nuts, finely chopped, for coating (optional)

Colored sprinkles, for coating (optional)

Shredded coconut, for coating (optional)

Crushed peppermint candies, for coating (optional)

1 Place the chocolate chips and milk in a microwave-safe bowl and microwave for 1 minute. Remove the bowl from the microwave, stir, and then microwave the mixture in 15-second intervals until the chocolate is almost melted, stirring after each interval.

2 Remove the bowl from the microwave and stir until the mixture is completely smooth. Add the butter and vanilla and stir until the mixture is smooth.

3 Place plastic wrap directly on the surface of the mixture and chill it in the refrigerator for 4 hours.

4 Line a baking sheet with parchment paper. Using a cookie scoop, form the chocolate mixture into balls and roll them in your desired coating(s).

5 Place the truffles on the baking sheet and store them in the refrigerator until ready to serve. Let the truffles come to room temperature before serving.

Cotton Candy Board

- **COTTON CANDY PUPPY CHOW (SEE PAGE 212)**

- **NO-BAKE CHEESECAKES (SEE PAGE 210)**

- **COTTON CANDY OREO BALLS (SEE PAGE 213)**

- **COTTON CANDY**

- **COTTON CANDY OREOS**

- **PINK POCKY**

- **ASSORTED PINK CANDIES**

- **ASSORTED BLUE CANDIES**

1   Choose a board, arrange all of the items on it in the desired manner, and enjoy.

A board that proves not every spread needs to be confined to a flat surface—in order to make sure all of the brightly colored confections here are looking their best, a tiered tray makes the most sense, as it lends a bit of necessary space to the proceedings and keeps the eyes from getting overwhelmed. This board also provides the recipe for one of the great sweet snacks in the world— Puppy Chow. Known in some corners as muddy buddies, it is always a good idea to have the ingredients required to make this crunchy delight on hand.

No-Bake Cheesecakes

Yield: 8 to 10 Mini Cakes / Active Time: 35 Minutes / Total Time: 3 Hours and 35 Minutes

½ lb. cream cheese, softened

⅓ cup sugar

1 teaspoon desired flavoring (cotton candy, vanilla extract, almond extract, etc.)

1 cup Cool Whip, thawed

4 graham crackers

Colored sprinkles, for topping (optional)

1   In the work bowl of a stand mixer fitted with the paddle attachment, beat the cream cheese until fluffy, about 3 minutes.

2   Add the sugar and beat to incorporate. Add the flavoring and beat to incorporate. Add the Cool Whip and fold to incorporate.

3   Transfer the mixture to a clean bowl, cover it with plastic wrap, and chill the filling in the refrigerator for 3 hours.

4   Crush the graham crackers and place 1 to 2 teaspoons in the bottom of your chosen containers. Place the filling in a piping bag fitted with a plain tip and pipe on top of the graham crackers. Top the cheesecakes with colored sprinkles (if desired) and serve.

Cotton Candy Puppy Chow

Yield: 12 Cups / Active Time: 35 Minutes / Total Time: 1 Hour and 5 Minutes

12 cups Rice Chex

⅔ cup pink chocolate melting wafers

2 teaspoons cotton candy flavoring

6 tablespoons confectioners' sugar

Colored sprinkles, to taste

⅔ cup blue chocolate melting wafers

1 Line two large baking sheets with parchment paper.

2 Place half of the cereal in a large mixing bowl.

3 Place the pink chocolate wafers in a microwave-safe bowl and microwave for 1 minute. Remove the bowl from the microwave, stir, and then microwave in 15-second intervals until the chocolate is almost melted, stirring after each interval. Remove the chocolate from the microwave and stir until smooth.

4 Stir 1 teaspoon of the cotton candy flavoring into the chocolate.

5 Pour the chocolate over the cereal and toss to coat.

6 Sprinkle half of the confectioners' sugar over the cereal and toss to coat.

7 Spread the cereal in an even layer on one of the baking sheets, add colored sprinkles, and let the puppy chow set for 15 minutes.

8 Repeat Steps 2 to 7 with the remaining cereal, the blue chocolate wafers, the remaining cotton candy flavoring and confectioners' sugar, and colored sprinkles.

9 Combine the two colors of puppy chow in a large bowl and serve.

Note: For a classic puppy chow, omit the cotton candy flavoring and use milk chocolate and white chocolate melting wafers.

Cotton Candy Oreo Balls

Yield: 28 Balls / Active Time: 40 Minutes / Total Time: 4 Hours and 20 Minutes

1 (20 oz.) package of Cotton Candy Oreos

½ lb. cream cheese, softened

1 lb. vanilla-flavored coating chocolate

¼ lb. pink chocolate melting wafers, for drizzling

¼ lb. blue chocolate melting wafers, for drizzling

Colored sprinkles, for topping

1 Line a baking sheet with parchment paper. Place the Oreos in a food processor and pulse until they are crushed. Add half of the cream cheese, pulse to incorporate, and then add the remaining cream cheese. Pulse to incorporate, making sure that the mixture is well combined enough to form it into balls. Form the mixture into balls, place them on the baking sheet, and chill them in the refrigerator for 3 hours.

2 Line a large baking sheet with parchment paper. Break the coating chocolate into squares and place them in a microwave-safe bowl. Microwave for 1 minute. Remove the bowl from the microwave, stir, and then microwave in 15-second intervals until the chocolate is almost melted, stirring after each interval. Remove the bowl from the microwave and stir until the chocolate is smooth.

3 Remove 4 to 6 balls from the refrigerator at a time. Secure the balls with two forks and dip them into the melted chocolate until they are completely coated. Place them on the baking sheet and let the chocolate sit until it has set, about 20 minutes.

4 Place the chocolate wafers in separate microwave-safe bowls and microwave for 1 minute. Remove the bowls from the microwave, stir, and then microwave in 15-second intervals until the chocolate is almost melted, stirring after each interval. Remove the bowls from the microwave and stir until the chocolate is smooth. Drizzle the chocolate over the balls, decorate them with sprinkles, and let the chocolate set for 15 minutes before serving or storing in the refrigerator.

Cotton Candy Puppy Chow, see page 212

Cupcake Fondue Board

- **1 TO 2 CONTAINERS OF STORE-BOUGHT VANILLA FROSTING**

- **2 TO 3 DROPS OF FOOD COLORING**

- **VANILLA CUPCAKES (SEE PAGE 218)**

- **CLASSIC CHOCOLATE BARK (SEE PAGE 202)**

- **FLAVORED TWIZZLERS**

- **DUM-DUMS**

- **SALTWATER TAFFY**

- **MIKE AND IKE CANDIES**

- **SKITTLES**

- **TOOTSIE POP DROPS**

1 Place the frosting and food coloring in a microwave-safe bowl and stir to combine. Place the frosting in the microwave, microwave until it is spreadable, about 15 seconds, and remove it from the microwave. Stir the frosting until smooth.

2 Choose a board, arrange the frosting and remaining items on it in the desired manner, and enjoy.

Yes, cupcakes are fun to begin with. But when you repurpose the conceit behind everyone's favorite retro party treat—fondue—and swap the cheese and bread out for frosting and cupcakes, you've really tapped into an exciting idea. Flank your cupcakes and frostings with plenty of colorful candies, and all of a sudden you've got a magical board with minimal effort.

Vanilla Cupcakes

Yield: 12 Cupcakes / Active Time: 25 Minutes / Total Time: 1 Hour

1¼ cups all-purpose flour

1¼ teaspoons baking powder

½ teaspoon baking soda

½ teaspoon kosher salt

2 large eggs, at room temperature

¾ cup sugar

½ cup canola oil

1½ teaspoons pure vanilla extract

½ cup buttermilk

1   Preheat the oven to 350°F. Line the wells of a muffin or cupcake pan with paper liners.

2   In a mixing bowl, whisk the flour, baking powder, baking soda, and salt to combine. Set the mixture aside.

3   In the work bowl of a stand mixer fitted with the whisk attachment, whip the eggs until lightly frothy.

4   Gradually add the sugar and whip to incorporate.

5   Fit the mixer with the paddle attachment. Add the canola oil and vanilla and beat to combine. Gradually add the dry mixture and buttermilk, alternating between them. Beat until the mixture comes together as a smooth, thin batter.

6   Divide the batter among the paper liners, filling each two-thirds of the way.

7   Place the cupcakes in the oven and bake until a toothpick inserted into their centers comes out clean, 12 to 15 minutes.

8   Remove the cupcakes from the oven and let them cool completely before serving.

Note: If you want smaller cupcakes for this board, the batter will make approximately 24 miniature cupcakes.

Dessert for Two Board

- **CHOCOLATE FONDUE (SEE PAGE 222)**

- **STRAWBERRIES**

- **PINEAPPLE**

- **APPLE SLICES**

- **BLUEBERRIES**

- **RASPBERRIES**

- **PRETZELS**

- **RICE KRISPIES TREATS**

- **MARSHMALLOWS**

- **COOKIE STICKS**

- **LONG WAFER SANDWICH COOKIES**

1   Choose a board, arrange all of the items on it in the desired manner, and enjoy.

When it's time for you and your dearest to take a step back and reconnect, turn to this board. The Chocolate Fondue that sits at the center of this spread is a good reminder that you don't need to overcomplicate things or work yourself to the bone when something special is called for—requiring only two ingredients and 15 minutes of your time, it's one of the simplest preparations in the book.

Chocolate Fondue

Yield: 2 Cups / Active Time: 15 Minutes / Total Time: 15 Minutes

1 (14 oz.) can of sweetened condensed milk   **1½ cups chocolate chips**

1   Place the ingredients in a small saucepan and cook over medium-low heat, stirring until the chocolate has melted and the mixture is smooth.

2   Transfer the mixture to a fondue pot and serve immediately.

- SNACK-SIZE BAGS OF ANIMAL CRACKERS

- COOKIES & CREAM PUDDING

- SNACK-SIZE BAGS OF OREOS

- WHIPPED CREAM, FOR TOPPING

- VANILLA PUDDING

- SNACK-SIZE BAGS OF CHIPS AHOY

- BANANA PUDDING

- SNACK-SIZE BAGS OF NILLA WAFERS

- BANANAS, SLICED, FOR TOPPING

- CHOCOLATE PUDDING

- SNACK-SIZE BAGS OF TEDDY GRAHAMS

- MINIATURE MARSHMALLOWS, FOR TOPPING

- CHOCOLATE CHIPS, FOR TOPPING

Dessert on the Go Basket

1   Choose a basket and place the bags of animal crackers in it. Open the remaining snack-size bags and dump the contents into bowls, making sure to keep each item together.

2   Place the cookies & cream pudding in the Oreo bags, top each portion with the Oreos and whipped cream, and place them in the basket. Place the vanilla pudding in the Chips Ahoy bags, top each portion with the Chips Ahoy and whipped cream, and place them in the basket.

3   Place the banana pudding in the Nilla Wafers bags, top each portion with the Nilla Wafers and bananas, and place them in the basket.

4   Place the chocolate pudding in the Teddy Grahams bags, top each portion with the Teddy Grahams, marshmallows, and chocolate chips, place them in the basket, and enjoy.

Need some on-the-go treats for an outdoor concert, sporting event, or party? By confining these desserts to individual bags, they become much easier to transport, both to the event and around it, as you mingle and catch up with the other attendees. By leveraging items purchased from the store, they are also very simple to put together, allowing you to get out the door and on to the fun.

Doughnut Board

- **VANILLA GLAZE (SEE PAGE 228)**

- **CHOCOLATE GLAZE (SEE PAGE 230)**

- **STRAWBERRY GLAZE (SEE PAGE 231)**

- **PEANUT BUTTER GLAZE (SEE PAGE 232)**

- **CARAMEL GLAZE (SEE PAGE 233)**

- **DOUGHNUTS**

- **FRUITY CEREAL, FOR TOPPING**

- **MINIATURE CHOCOLATE CANDIES, FOR TOPPING**

- **COLORED SPRINKLES, FOR TOPPING**

- **CHOCOLATE SANDWICH COOKIES, CRUMBLED, FOR TOPPING**

- **PECANS, CHOPPED, FOR TOPPING**

1   Apply the glazes to the doughnuts, dipping their tops into the glazes. Top the vanilla-glazed doughnuts with fruity cereal, the chocolate-glazed doughnuts with chocolate candies, the strawberry-glazed doughnuts with colored sprinkles, the peanut butter–glazed doughnuts with crumbled chocolate sandwich cookies, and the caramel-glazed doughnuts with pecans.

2   Choose a board, arrange the doughnuts on it in the desired manner, and enjoy.

Don't settle for what the local shop decides should be on your doughnuts. Instead, grab a dozen some Saturday morning, whip up this group of glazes, and spend the rest of the weekend tailoring them to suit your taste. And avoid spending too much time thinking about which toppings should be included—this is one of those instances where the old adage of "the more the merrier" proves to be true.

Vanilla Glaze

Yield: Glaze for 12 to 24 Doughnuts / Active Time: 5 Minutes / Total Time: 5 Minutes

1 cup confectioners' sugar

1 tablespoon whole milk, plus more as needed

1 teaspoon clear vanilla extract

1 Place all of the ingredients in a mixing bowl and whisk until the mixture is smooth and has the desired consistency. If the glaze is too thick, incorporate more milk.

Chocolate Glaze

Yield: Glaze for 12 to 24 Doughnuts / Active Time: 5 Minutes / Total Time: 5 Minutes

1 cup sifted confectioners' sugar

¼ cup unsweetened cocoa powder

3 tablespoons whole milk, plus more as needed

1 teaspoon pure vanilla extract

1   Place all of the ingredients in a mixing bowl and whisk until the mixture is smooth and has the desired consistency. If the glaze is too thick, incorporate more milk.

Strawberry Glaze

Yield: Glaze for 12 to 24 Doughnuts / Active Time: 5 Minutes / Total Time: 5 Minutes

¾ cup sifted confectioners' sugar

3 tablespoons pureed strawberries, plus more as needed

1 Place the ingredients in a mixing bowl and whisk until the mixture is smooth and has the desired consistency. If the glaze is too thick, incorporate more pureed strawberries.

Peanut Butter Glaze

Yield: Glaze for 12 to 24 Doughnuts / Active Time: 5 Minutes / Total Time: 5 Minutes

6 tablespoons peanut butter

2 tablespoons unsalted butter, melted

2 tablespoons confectioners' sugar

1 Place the ingredients in a mixing bowl and whisk until the mixture is smooth and has the desired consistency.

Caramel Glaze

Yield: Glaze for 12 to 24 Doughnuts / Active Time: 20 Minutes / Total Time: 30 Minutes

1 cup packed light brown sugar

6 tablespoons unsalted butter

1 cup heavy cream

1 teaspoon pure vanilla extract

1   Combine all of the ingredients in a small saucepan and cook over medium heat, swirling the pan occasionally.

2   Cook until the mixture thickens slightly, about 10 minutes. Remove the pan from heat and let the glaze cool completely.

Frosting Board

- **FUNFETTI FROSTING (SEE PAGE 236)**
- **OREOS**
- **FUDGE STRIPE COOKIES**
- **ANIMAL CRACKERS**
- **NILLA WAFERS**
- **LONG SANDWICH WAFER COOKIES**
- **STRAWBERRIES**
- **PRETZELS**
- **CHOCOLATE-COVERED PRETZELS**
- **SHORTBREAD**
- **CHOCOLATE CHIP COOKIES**
- **GRAHAM CRACKER STICKS**
- **COLORED SPRINKLES**

1 Choose a board, arrange all of the items on it in the desired manner, and enjoy.

If you've been neglecting your inner child for some time, this board is an opportunity to fully embrace it, being so sweet and easy to put together that it feels positively mischievous. Though the frosting here is homemade, don't feel like that is a requirement; store-bought frosting will work just as well. The important thing is the dipping options, as you want to make sure that everyone's faves are included.

Funfetti Frosting

Yield: 6 Cups / Active Time: 15 Minutes / Total Time: 15 Minutes

1 cup unsalted butter, softened

4 to 5 cups sifted confectioners' sugar

3 to 4 tablespoons whole milk

1 teaspoon clear vanilla extract

⅔ cup rainbow sprinkles

1   In the work bowl of a stand mixer fitted with the paddle attachment, beat the butter until it is fluffy, 5 to 6 minutes.

2   With the mixer running, alternate adding 1 cup of confectioners' sugar and 1 tablespoon of milk until the frosting has the desired consistency. Add the vanilla and sprinkles and beat until they are evenly distributed. Use immediately or store the frosting in the refrigerator until ready to use.

3   If the frosting is chilled, let it come to room temperature before using.

Game Night Board

- **SWEET & SALTY SNACK MIX (SEE PAGE 240)**

- **CHOCOLATE & PEANUT BUTTER BARK (SEE PAGE 242)**

- **CAKE BATTER POPCORN (SEE PAGE 192)**

- **RICE KRISPIES TREATS**

1   Choose a board, arrange all of the items on it in the desired manner, and enjoy.

No doubt, everyone loves playing the games that game night is built around, but let's be honest: the snacks are what really bring everyone together. This collection of confections is no doubt a step up from the typical spread, and it is also mindful that when you're playing games, the most important thing is keeping everyone's hands from becoming too sticky.

Sweet & Salty Snack Mix

Yield: 8 Cups / Active Time: 10 Minutes / Total Time: 10 Minutes

4 cups Rice Chex

4 cups Golden Grahams

¾ lb. dried cranberries

7 oz. vanilla yogurt raisins

1 (14¾ oz.) can of mixed nuts

1 Place all of the ingredients in a large bowl, stir to combine, and serve.

Chocolate & Peanut Butter Bark

Yield: 10 Servings / Active Time: 10 Minutes / Total Time: 35 Minutes

1½ lbs. coating chocolate

1 cup peanut butter chips

1 tablespoon creamy peanut butter

Miniature peanut butter cups, halved, for topping (optional)

Reese's Pieces, for topping (optional)

Pretzels, broken into pieces, for topping (optional)

Peanuts, chopped, for topping (optional)

1 Line a large baking sheet with parchment paper. Break the coating chocolate into squares and place them in a microwave-safe bowl. Microwave for 1 minute. Remove the bowl from the microwave, stir, and then microwave in 15-second intervals until the chocolate is almost melted, stirring after each interval. Remove the bowl from the microwave and stir until the chocolate is smooth.

2 Pour the chocolate into the baking sheet and spread it with an offset spatula, making sure that it is even.

3 Place the peanut butter chips and peanut butter in a clean microwave-safe bowl. Microwave for 1 minute. Remove the bowl from the microwave, stir, and then microwave in 15-second intervals until the peanut butter chips are almost melted, stirring after each interval. Remove the bowl from the microwave and stir until the mixture is smooth.

4 Add spoonfuls of the peanut butter mixture to the melted chocolate and swirl with a knife.

5 Distribute any toppings over the chocolate-and-peanut butter mixture and let it sit until it has set, about 20 minutes.

6 Break the bark into pieces and serve or store in an airtight container.

Honey Bee Board

- **HONEYCOMB WAFFLES**

- **HONEY & CINNAMON BUTTER**

- **LEMON CANDIES**

- **BUTTER WAFFLE COOKIES**

- **BIT-O-HONEY CANDIES**

- **HONEYCOMB CEREAL**

- **HONEY STICKS**

- **HONEY SPOONS**

1   Choose a board, arrange all of the items on it in the desired manner, and enjoy.

You'll have everyone buzzing with this spread. Leveraging the irresistible sweetness of honey for all that it is worth, this is a light and bright-tasting board that will bring a smile to everyone's face. A special waffle maker is needed for the honeycomb waffles, but considering all of the nooks they have for something sweet to settle in, it's a worthy investment.

Honey Bee Board, see page 243

Harry Potter Board

- **PRETZEL STICKS**

- **HOMEMADE PEANUT BUTTER CUPS (SEE PAGE 136)**

- **FLAVORED POPCORN (SEE PAGE 248)**

- **PUMPKIN HAND PIES (SEE PAGE 250)**

- **CHOCOLATE AND CARAMEL–DIPPED PRETZEL WANDS**

- **CHOCOLATE FROGS**

- **CHOCOLATE COINS**

- **JELLY SLUGS**

- **JELLY BEANS**

- **HARRY POTTER HERSHEY KISSES**

1   Stick pretzel sticks into the bottoms of the Homemade Peanut Butter Cups, making them look like broomsticks.

2   Choose a board, arrange the broomsticks and other items on it in the desired manner, and enjoy.

Got a family full of Potterphiles? Plan to make this board for your next sprint through the incredible series of movies that were made from the books. Filled with pretzel wands and broomsticks, it's a great spread to enjoy as you argue over which house everyone belongs to: Gryffindor, Hufflepuff, Ravenclaw, or Slytherin.

Flavored Popcorn

Yield: 12 Cups / Active Time: 30 Minutes / Total Time: 1 Hour

12 cups popped popcorn

¼ cup honey

½ cup unsalted butter

½ cup sugar

1 (3 oz.) box of Jell-O

1   Preheat the oven to 250°F.

2   Line two large baking sheets with parchment paper. Place the popcorn in a large bowl and set it aside.

3   In a medium saucepan, combine the honey and butter and warm the mixture over medium heat until the butter has melted.

4   In a small bowl, combine the sugar and Jell-O. Stir the sugar mixture into the saucepan, bring the mixture to a gentle boil, and cook for 4 to 5 minutes.

5   Pour the mixture over the popcorn and gently toss to coat.

6   Spread the popcorn on the baking sheets and place them in the oven.

7   Bake the popcorn for 30 minutes, stirring every 10 minutes. Remove the popcorn from the oven and let it cool. Break the popcorn apart and serve.

Pumpkin Hand Pies

Yield: 8 Hand Pies / Active Time: 35 Minutes / Total Time: 1 Hour and 30 Minutes

¾ cup pumpkin puree

¼ cup packed light brown sugar

½ teaspoon cinnamon

½ teaspoon pumpkin pie spice

¼ teaspoon freshly grated nutmeg

¼ teaspoon ground ginger

1 (14.1 oz.) Pillsbury Ready to Bake Pie Crusts

All-purpose flour, as needed

1 large egg

1 tablespoon water

Turbinado sugar, for topping

1   Preheat the oven to 350°F.

2   Line a baking sheet with parchment paper or a silicone mat.

3   In a mixing bowl, whisk together the pumpkin puree, brown sugar, cinnamon, pumpkin pie spice, nutmeg, and ginger. Set the mixture aside.

4   Place the pie crusts on a flour-dusted work surface and roll them out. Using a pumpkin-shaped cookie cutter, cut the crusts into 16 pieces. Top half of the crusts with about ¼ cup of the filling.

5   Top each pie with a crust and press down on the edges of the hand pies to seal them. In a small bowl, whisk together the egg and water.

6   Brush the hand pies with the egg wash, sprinkle turbinado sugar over them, and place them on the baking sheet.

7   Place the pies in the oven and bake until they are golden brown, 10 to 12 minutes. Remove the hand pies from the oven, transfer them to a wire rack, and let them cool completely before serving.

Movie Night Board

- **COOKIE PIZZA (SEE PAGE 254)**

- **M&M COOKIES (SEE PAGE 256)**

- **POPCORN**

- **ASSORTED CANDIES**

- **ASSORTED COOKIES**

1 Choose a board, arrange all of the items on it in the desired manner, and enjoy.

Instead of heading out to the theater and getting gouged by the excessive prices they charge for treats, use this board to create an even better selection in the comfort of your own home. With the Cookie Pizza and M&M Cookies standing at the center, and your all-time favorites from the concession stand around them, you're guaranteed to have a blockbuster evening.

Cookie Pizza

Yield: 10 to 12 Servings / Active Time: 25 Minutes / Total Time: 1 Hour and 30 Minutes

1 To begin preparations for the pizza, preheat the oven to 350°F.

2 Coat a round 12-inch pan (you want a pan that is at least ½ inch deep) with nonstick cooking spray.

3 In the work bowl of a stand mixer fitted with the paddle attachment, cream together the butter, brown sugar, milk, and vanilla until the mixture is smooth and fluffy.

4 Add the egg and beat to incorporate.

5 In a small bowl, whisk together the flour, salt, and baking soda.

6 Add the mixture to the work bowl and beat until the mixture comes together as a smooth dough. Add the chocolate chips and beat until they are evenly distributed.

7 Spread the mixture evenly over the pan, leaving about ½ inch around the edge. Place the pan in the oven and cook until the edge of the cookie is golden brown, 15 to 20 minutes.

8 Remove the cookie from the oven, transfer it to a wire rack, and let it cool completely.

9 To prepare the topping, clean out the work bowl, add the cream cheese, and beat until it is fluffy, 3 to 4 minutes.

10 Add the confectioners' sugar and vanilla and beat until the mixture is creamy. Add the Cool Whip, fold to incorporate, and spread the topping over the cookie. Top the cookie with candies and colored sprinkles, slice it, and serve.

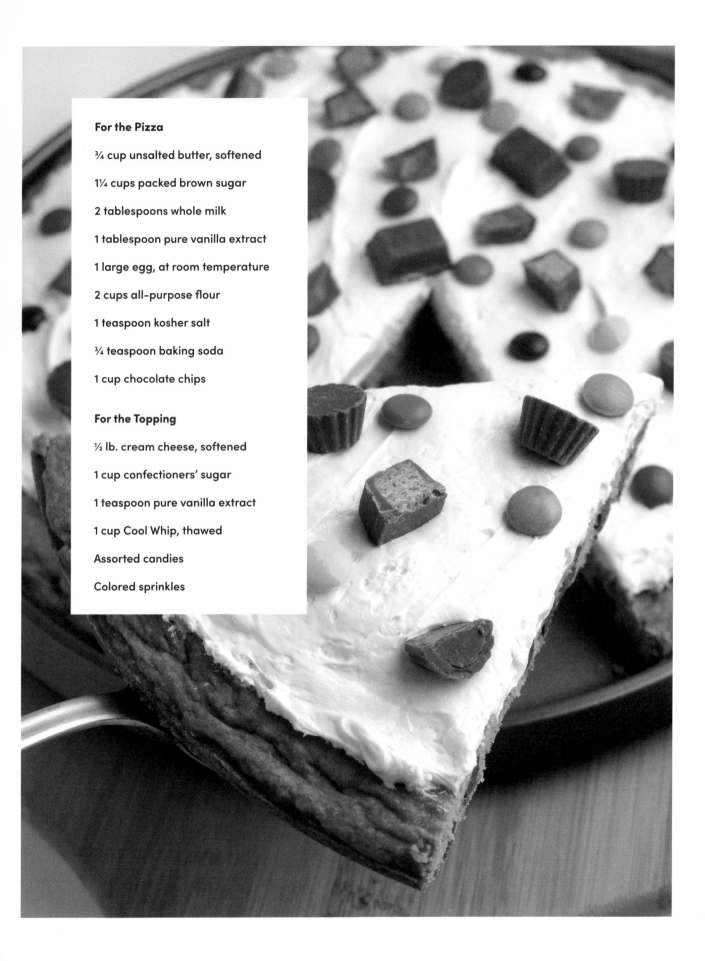

For the Pizza

¾ cup unsalted butter, softened

1¼ cups packed brown sugar

2 tablespoons whole milk

1 tablespoon pure vanilla extract

1 large egg, at room temperature

2 cups all-purpose flour

1 teaspoon kosher salt

¾ teaspoon baking soda

1 cup chocolate chips

For the Topping

½ lb. cream cheese, softened

1 cup confectioners' sugar

1 teaspoon pure vanilla extract

1 cup Cool Whip, thawed

Assorted candies

Colored sprinkles

M&M Cookies

Yield: 36 Cookies / Active Time: 25 Minutes / Total Time: 1 Hour and 30 Minutes

1 Preheat the oven to 375°F. Line two baking sheets with parchment paper or silicone mats.

2 In a mixing bowl, whisk together the flour, salt, and baking soda. Set the mixture aside.

3 In the work bowl of a stand mixer fitted with the paddle attachment, cream together the butter, pudding mix, brown sugar, sugar, and vanilla until the mixture is light and fluffy.

4 Add the eggs and beat to incorporate them.

5 Gradually add the flour mixture and beat until the mixture comes together as a smooth dough.

6 Add the M&M'S and chocolate chips and beat until they are evenly distributed.

7 Form the dough into balls, place them on the baking sheets, and gently press down on them to flatten them slightly.

8 Place more M&M'S on top of the cookies, place them in the oven, and bake until they are lightly golden brown, 8 to 10 minutes.

9 Remove the cookies from the oven and let them cool briefly on the baking sheets before transferring them to a wire rack. Let them cool completely before serving.

2¼ cups all-purpose flour

1 teaspoon kosher salt

1 teaspoon baking soda

1 cup unsalted butter, softened

1 (3.4 oz.) box of instant vanilla
pudding

¾ cup packed brown sugar

¼ cup sugar

1 teaspoon pure vanilla extract

2 eggs, at room temperature

¾ lb. M&M'S

1 cup chocolate chips

Nostalgic Board

- **WHOOPIE PIES (SEE PAGE 260)**
- **COSMIC BROWNIES**
- **SNICKERDOODLES (SEE PAGE 262)**
- **ASSORTED RETRO CANDIES**
- **OATMEAL CREAM PIES**

1   Choose a board, arrange all of the items on it in the desired manner, and enjoy.

When it comes to sweets, we all have those extra-sweet treats that we can't help looking back with fondness at, even if we're nowhere near as driven by getting our sugar fix as we once were. This board gathers all of those old-school confections together, allowing you to relive those exhilarating trips to the corner store when you had a few dollars in your pocket and the potential for enjoyment seemed limitless.

Whoopie Pies

Yield: 14 to 16 Pies / Active Time: 30 Minutes / Total Time: 1 Hour and 45 Minutes

1   To begin preparations for the pies, preheat the oven to 350°F.

2   Line two baking sheets with parchment paper or silicone mats.

3   In a medium bowl, whisk together the flour, baking cocoa, baking soda, baking powder, and salt. Set the mixture aside.

4   In the work bowl of a stand mixer fitted with the paddle attachment, beat the sugar and canola oil until thoroughly combined.

5   Add the eggs, milk, and vanilla and beat until the mixture is smooth.

6   Gradually add the dry mixture and beat until the mixture comes together as a smooth dough.

7   Form the dough into ½ oz. balls, place them on the baking sheets, and gently press down on the balls to flatten them slightly. Place the pies in the oven and bake until the edges are set but still soft, 7 to 10 minutes.

8   Remove the pies from the oven and let them cool on the baking sheets for 5 minutes. Transfer the pies to a wire rack and let them cool completely.

9   To begin preparations for the filling, wipe out the work bowl, add the butter and confectioners' sugar, and beat until the mixture is light and fluffy, about 5 minutes.

10 Add the vanilla and salt and beat to incorporate. Add the marshmallow creme and fold to incorporate. Chill the filling in the refrigerator for 30 minutes.

11 Place the filling in a piping bag fitted with a large round tip and pipe the filling onto the bottoms of half of the pies. Top the filling with the remaining pies and serve immediately.

For the Pies

1¾ cups all-purpose flour

¾ cup unsweetened baking cocoa

2 teaspoons baking soda

½ teaspoon baking powder

½ teaspoon kosher salt

1 cup sugar

½ cup canola oil

2 large eggs, at room temperature

¼ cup whole milk

1 teaspoon pure vanilla extract

For the Filling

1 cup unsalted butter, softened

1 cup confectioners' sugar

2 teaspoons pure vanilla extract

¼ teaspoon fine sea salt

1¼ cups marshmallow creme

Snickerdoodles

Yield: 36 to 40 Cookies / Active Time: 25 Minutes / Total Time: 1 Hour and 30 Minutes

2¾ cups all-purpose flour

2 teaspoons cream of tartar

1 teaspoon baking soda

½ teaspoon kosher salt

1 cup unsalted butter, softened

1½ cups plus ¼ cup sugar

2 large eggs, at room temperature

2 tablespoons whole milk

1 teaspoon pure vanilla extract

2 teaspoons cinnamon

1   Preheat the oven to 350°F.

2   Line two baking sheets with parchment paper or silicone mats. In a medium bowl, whisk together the flour, cream of tartar, baking soda, and salt. Set the mixture aside.

3   In the work bowl of a stand mixer fitted with the paddle attachment, beat the butter and 1½ cups sugar until the mixture is light and fluffy, 4 to 5 minutes.

4   Add the eggs, milk, and vanilla and beat until the mixture is smooth. Gradually add the dry mixture and beat until the mixture comes together as a smooth dough.

5   In a small bowl, whisk together the remaining sugar and the cinnamon.

6   Form the dough into balls, roll them in the cinnamon sugar, and place them on the baking sheets. Place the cookies in the oven and bake until the edges are set and the centers are still soft, 8 to 10 minutes.

7   Remove the cookies from the oven, transfer them to a wire rack, and let them cool completely before serving.

Princess Board

- **STRAWBERRY FUDGE (SEE PAGE 266)**

- **STRAWBERRY CREAM PIES (SEE PAGE 268)**

- **ASSORTED PINK CANDIES**

- **PINK MOONPIES**

- **PINK SNOWBALLS**

- **PINK POCKY**

1 Choose a board, arrange all of the items on it in the desired manner, and enjoy.

We all know that one princess who can't have enough pink in their life, and this board is a fitting celebration for these folks. Built around the luscious Strawberry Fudge and easy-to-make-but-oh-so-elegant Strawberry Cream Pies, your queen of the scene will feel very seen after just a few bites from this spread.

Strawberry Fudge

Yield: 36 Pieces / Active Time: 25 Minutes / Total Time: 3 Hours and 25 Minutes

¾ lb. white chocolate chips

2 cups strawberry frosting

Pink sprinkles, for topping (optional)

1 Line a square 8-inch baking pan with parchment paper, making sure that it hangs over the sides of the pan.

2 Place the chocolate chips in a microwave-safe bowl and microwave for 1 minute. Remove the bowl from the microwave, stir, and then microwave in 15-second intervals until the chocolate chips are almost melted, stirring after each interval. Remove the bowl from the microwave and stir until the chocolate chips are smooth.

3 Add the frosting to the melted chocolate and stir until the mixture is completely smooth. Spread the mixture evenly in the baking pan. Top the fudge with the sprinkles (if desired) and gently press down on them so that they adhere.

4 Place the fudge in the refrigerator and chill until it is set, about 3 hours.

5 Use the parchment paper to remove the fudge from the pan, cut it into squares, and serve.

Strawberry Cream Pies

Yield: 10 to 12 Mini Pies / Active Time: 30 Minutes / Total Time: 3 Hours and 30 Minutes

1 (3 oz.) box of strawberry gelatin

½ cup boiling water

½ cup cold water

1 cup Cool Whip, thawed

1 cup chopped strawberries, plus more for topping

4 graham crackers, crushed

1 In a large bowl, stir together the gelatin and boiling water until the gelatin has dissolved, 2 to 3 minutes.

2 Stir in the cold water until thoroughly incorporated. Add the Cool Whip and fold to incorporate. Add the strawberries and stir until they are evenly distributed. Place the filling in the refrigerator to set for at least 2 hours.

3 Remove the filling from the refrigerator. Add 1 to 2 teaspoons of graham cracker crumbs to your miniature serving containers and spoon the filling over the top. Top with additional strawberries and serve the pies immediately or store them in the refrigerator.

Note: This recipe can easily be made into a large pie by using a store-bought graham cracker crust. If you do, chill the pie in the refrigerator for 3 hours after placing the filling in the crust.

Quick Bread Board

- **LEMON & RASPBERRY QUICK BREAD (SEE PAGE 272)**

- **PUMPKIN & CHOCOLATE QUICK BREAD (SEE PAGE 274)**

- **BANANA BREAD**

- **CINNAMON BUTTER**

- **APPLE BUTTER**

- **CREAM CHEESE**

1   Choose a board, arrange all of the items on it in the desired manner, and enjoy.

Here's a great board to prepare when you have family coming in for the weekend, as you can spend the day before baking the loaves, put them out once everyone arrives, and let everyone graze and nibble as they please throughout the weekend. The quick bread recipes provided here are just one option—please feel free to swap them out for your favorites, or for whatever ingredients you have on hand already.

Lemon & Raspberry Quick Bread

Yield: 1 Loaf / Active Time: 30 Minutes / Total Time: 3 Hours and 35 Minutes

1¾ cups all-purpose flour

1¼ teaspoons baking powder

½ teaspoon kosher salt

½ cup unsalted butter, softened

¾ cup sugar

2 large eggs

1½ teaspoons pure vanilla extract

¾ cup milk

Zest of 1 lemon

⅓ cup raspberry jam, warm

1   Preheat the oven to 350°F.

2   Line a 9 x 5–inch loaf pan with parchment paper. In a small bowl, whisk together the flour, baking powder, and salt. Set the mixture aside.

3   In the work bowl of a stand mixer fitted with the paddle attachment, beat the butter and sugar until the mixture is fluffy. Add the eggs and vanilla and beat to incorporate. Add the milk and lemon zest and beat to incorporate.

4   Add the dry mixture and beat until the mixture just comes together as a smooth batter, making sure not to overmix. Pour the batter into the loaf pan, add small spoonfuls of the jam to the batter, and swirl them with a knife.

5   Place the bread in the oven and bake until a toothpick inserted into the center comes out clean, 55 minutes to 1 hour.

6   Remove the bread from the oven and let it cool in the pan for 1 hour.

7   Remove the bread from the pan, transfer it to a wire rack, and let it cool completely before serving.

Pumpkin & Chocolate Quick Bread

Yield: 2 Loaves / Active Time: 25 Minutes / Total Time: 3 Hours and 45 Minutes

1 To begin preparations for the pumpkin batter, preheat the oven to 350°F.

2 Coat two 9 x 5–inch loaf pans with nonstick cooking spray and dust them with flour, knocking out any excess. In a mixing bowl, whisk together the flour, baking powder, baking soda, salt, and spices. Set the mixture aside.

3 In the work bowl of a stand mixer fitted with the paddle attachment, beat the sugar and canola oil until the mixture is thoroughly combined.

4 Add the eggs and pumpkin and beat until well combined. Gradually add the dry mixture and beat until the mixture comes together as a smooth batter. Add the walnuts (if desired) and beat until they are evenly distributed. Set the pumpkin batter aside.

5 To begin preparations for the chocolate batter, place the flour, sugar, cocoa powder, chocolate chips, baking powder, salt, and baking soda in a mixing bowl and whisk to combine.

6 In a separate mixing bowl, whisk together the sour cream, canola oil, eggs, and vanilla. Add the mixture to the dry mixture and fold until thoroughly combined.

7 Add half of the pumpkin batter and half of the chocolate batter to each loaf pan.

8 Swirl the batters with a knife, place the pans in the oven, and bake until a toothpick inserted into the centers of the loaves comes out clean, 60 to 70 minutes.

9 Remove the loaves from the oven and let them cool in the pans for 1 hour.

10 Remove the loaves from the pans, transfer them to a wire rack, and let them cool completely before serving.

For the Pumpkin Batter

3 cups all-purpose flour, plus more as needed

½ teaspoon baking powder

1 teaspoon baking soda

½ teaspoon kosher salt

1 teaspoon ground cloves

1 teaspoon cinnamon

1 teaspoon freshly grated nutmeg

3 cups sugar

1 cup canola oil

3 large eggs, at room temperature

1 (15 oz.) can of pumpkin

1 cup chopped walnuts (optional)

For the Chocolate Batter

1½ cups all-purpose flour

¾ cup sugar

¼ cup unsweetened cocoa powder

¼ cup semisweet chocolate chips

1 teaspoon baking powder

½ teaspoon kosher salt

¼ teaspoon baking soda

1½ cups sour cream

½ cup canola oil

2 large eggs, at room temperature

1 teaspoon pure vanilla extract

Rainbow Board

- **FUNFETTI CAKE MIX COOKIE SANDWICHES (SEE PAGE 107 FOR THE COOKIES)**

- **FUNFETTI SHORTBREAD (SEE PAGE 198)**

- **FRUITY PEBBLES TREATS**

- **RAINBOW PUPPY CHOW (SEE PAGE 212)**

- **SNACK MIX**

- **COLORED SPRINKLES**

- **RAINBOW TWIZZLERS**

1 Choose a board, arrange all of the items on it in the desired manner, and enjoy.

If your crew is feeling down, make them this eye-catching board and watch how quickly things turn around. Bursting with brightly colored treats and filled with a heady array of flavors—moving from fruity and tart to rich and savory—this spread has the power to melt away all gray.

Slumber Party Board

- **SLEEPING BAG COOKIES (SEE PAGE 281)**
- **CHOCOLATE WAFFLES (SEE PAGE 280)**
- **MARSHMALLOW POPS**
- **CHOCOLATE-COVERED PRETZELS**
- **WHIPPED CREAM**
- **ASSORTED PINK AND PURPLE CANDIES**

1 Choose a board, arrange all of the items on it in the desired manner, and enjoy.

Those first sleepovers where your children have their friends stay the night are an extra-special rite of passage. Make the most of these momentous occasions by putting together this spread, making sure that you have a complete dossier on each of the guests so that you can make the Sleeping Bag Cookies resemble everyone at the party. Pull that off, and the group is guaranteed to have a great, unforgettable night.

Chocolate Waffles

Yield: 8 Servings / Active Time: 25 Minutes / Total Time: 45 Minutes

2¼ cups all-purpose flour

½ cup unsweetened cocoa powder

½ cup sugar

2 teaspoons baking powder

1 teaspoon baking soda

2 large eggs, separated

1 cup whole milk

½ cup canola oil

Strawberries, sliced, for serving

Chocolate Syrup (see page 62), for serving

Confectioners' sugar, for serving

1 In a large bowl, whisk the flour, cocoa powder, sugar, baking powder, and baking soda together. Set the mixture aside.

2 Place the egg whites in a bowl and set them aside. Add the milk, egg yolks, and canola oil to the dry mixture and whisk until the mixture comes together as a smooth batter.

3 Whisk the egg whites until they are very foamy, add them to the batter, and fold to incorporate.

4 Heat a waffle iron and coat it with nonstick cooking spray. Pour some batter into the waffle iron and cook until the waffle is cooked through, 5 to 8 minutes. Repeat with the remaining batter and serve the waffles with strawberries, Chocolate Syrup, and confectioners' sugar.

Sleeping Bag Cookies

Yield: 24 Cookies / Active Time: 20 Minutes / Total Time: 1 Hour

¼ lb. chocolate melting wafers

24 long wafer sandwich cookies

24 Nilla Wafers

Frosting, as needed

Food coloring, as needed

1 Line two baking sheets with parchment paper and place a wire rack in one of the baking sheets.

2 Place the chocolate wafers in a microwave-safe bowl and microwave for 1 minute. Remove the bowl from the microwave, stir, and then microwave in 15-second intervals until the chocolate is almost melted, stirring after each interval. Remove the bowl from the microwave and stir until the chocolate is smooth.

3 Dip the long wafer cookies into the melted chocolate until they are coated, letting any excess chocolate drip into the bowl. Place them on the wire rack and let the chocolate set.

4 Using a food writer pen, draw faces on the Nilla Wafers.

5 Warm the melted chocolate in the microwave and use it to attach the Nilla Wafers to the long wafer cookies. Review the guest list for the slumber party to determine how many different hair colors you want. Divide the frosting among that number of bowls, add the desired food coloring to each one, and stir to combine.

6 Transfer the frostings to piping bags fitted with round tips and pipe the hair onto the heads. Let the cookies set for 1 hour before serving.

Conversion Table

Weights

1 oz. = 28 grams
2 oz. = 57 grams
4 oz. (¼ lb.) = 113 grams
8 oz. (½ lb.) = 227 grams
16 oz. (1 lb.) = 454 grams

Volume Measures

⅛ teaspoon = 0.6 ml
¼ teaspoon = 1.23 ml
½ teaspoon = 2.5 ml
1 teaspoon = 5 ml
1 tablespoon (3 teaspoons) = ½ fluid oz. = 15 ml
2 tablespoons = 1 fluid oz. = 29.5 ml
¼ cup (4 tablespoons) = 2 fluid oz. = 59 ml
⅓ cup (5⅓ tablespoons) = 2.7 fluid oz. = 80 ml
½ cup (8 tablespoons) = 4 fluid oz. = 120 ml
⅔ cup (10⅔ tablespoons) = 5.4 fluid oz. = 160 ml
¾ cup (12 tablespoons) = 6 fluid oz. = 180 ml
1 cup (16 tablespoons) = 8 fluid oz. = 240 ml

Temperature Equivalents

°F	°C	Gas Mark
225	110	¼
250	130	½
275	140	1
300	150	2
325	170	3
350	180	4
375	190	5
400	200	6
425	220	7
450	230	8
475	240	9
500	250	10

Length Measures

1/16 inch = 1.6 mm
⅛ inch = 3 mm
¼ inch = 6.35 mm
½ inch = 1.25 cm
¾ inch = 2 cm
1 inch = 2.5 cm

Index

Acknowledgments

It is with much grace and gratitude that I thank you for choosing my book as a resource to help you build amazing dessert boards. Whether you want to keep it simple, or if you love a grand celebration, I believe that striving to be passionate about life is most important.

Thank you to my husband, Doug. Your help, love, and encouragement with this book and throughout our 35 years of marriage mean the world to me.

To my boys and their girls, thank you for always being there when I needed help in the kitchen, organizing the mounds of cookies and candy, and being willing to give me feedback on my ideas.

Henry, you will always be my little warrior. You bring joy and love to my life every single day. Nana loves you to the moon and back a million times. Shine bright, sugar.

Although my parents are no longer physically with me, I know they were watching and encouraging me every step I took, every cookie and piece of candy I placed on a board. And every photo I took. Thank you Mom and Dad, for teaching me how to be strong. I'm beyond grateful for the creativity you passed onto me.

And last, but certainly not least, thank you to the team at Cider Mill Press and HarperCollins. Thank you for answering my endless questions, for being patient with me and for allowing me to share my love for Dessert Boards with the world.

"It's not where you are in life, it's who you have by your side that matters."
—anonymous

About the Author

Born and raised in Indiana, Liz's roots run deep in Midwest homemaking. Her blog, Hoosier Homemade, began in 2009, based around a desire to share what she has learned through her love for creating charcuterie boards, baking, decorating, and making a house a home. She loves all the holidays and shares easy, creative ways to build memories with your family.

Liz is a wife, mom of three grown boys and two daughter-in-laws, and is a grandmother to her precious grandson.

She believes in doing what you love, inspiring others to do the same, that every day should be celebrated, and simply being together is often enough.

About Cider Mill Press Book Publishers

Good ideas ripen with time. From seed to harvest,
Cider Mill Press brings fine reading, information, and entertainment
together between the covers of its creatively crafted books.
Our Cider Mill bears fruit twice a year, publishing a new
crop of titles each spring and fall.

"Where Good Books Are Ready for Press"
501 Nelson Place
Nashville, Tennessee 37214

cidermillpress.com